14 Rules for Admissions Screening in Higher Ed

An Antidote to Bias

Behrouz Moemeni

SortSmart Candidate Selection Inc.

Table of Contents

Foreword:

Is it possible to create an admissions screening process that allows any educational institution to select top-performing applicants and simultaneously promote diversity? Is it possible to choose applicants genuinely motivated in the pursuit of a profession rather than those primarily focused on acquiring wealth or status? Is it possible to achieve all of the above, being fair to all applicants *and* reducing the time and cost of the admissions screening process?

These were the questions plaguing me in 2013. Since then, a lot has changed; I am now confident that the overarching answer is a resounding "yes!"

In this book, I will share the required steps to achieve all of the above considerations for your own admissions screening process.

If you are an admissions dean, director, officer, administrator, or researcher, this is the perfect book for both you and your team. If you are anyone interested to learn more about admissions screening in higher education, you are also going to enjoy this book.

I recommend that you read this book in the order it is presented because each chapter builds on the information provided by the preceding ones. The book is concise and easy to read with no fluff. I bet you can finish it from cover to cover in an afternoon.

I hope you enjoy this book as much as I enjoyed writing it for you. If you do, feel free to share it with others who may also benefit.

Lastly, I invite you to connect with me on my website (behrouzmoemeni.com) to share your valuable thoughts and comments.

Chapter I

Introduction

What do top performers such as Usain Bolt, Serena Williams, Albert Einstein, and Steve Jobs have in common? What allows them to reach *that* level of mastery in life? What makes them sustain their level of dedication, often for decades, despite many obstacles? Most importantly, how can we select such individuals during the university admissions process and simultaneously promote diversity?

Several years ago, a personal discovery provided me profound insight into such questions. It fundamentally changed the way I think about education, work, and life.

This book is about how I made the discovery and why it is essential—not just for university admissions screening, but in our daily work and lives.

On a gloomy Friday the 13th, in December 2013, I received my PhD in Immunology from the University of Toronto. This was a truly scary day. Not because I am superstitious, but because I was at a crossroads—take advantage of a lucrative job offer and continue in academia or go all in with my company, BeMo, which I had started mere months ago with little revenue to keep the lights on? The job offer would present a secure source of income and guaranteed career-advancement opportunity, allowing me to repay my hefty student loan. My fledgling company would earn me uncertainty, the fear of the unknown, added debt, the disapproval of my family, and a stomach ulcer. I chose the company, of course. It was a no-brainer.

Why would I do something that seemed so foolish at the time without any business training? I did not know the answer at the time; regardless, I was certain of continuing on this path. I could not bring myself to do anything else. There was an internal drive for the company that pulled me—I obsessed over it all the time. I worked 16-hour days. Sometimes I could not sleep at night, unable to stop thinking about what I wanted to accomplish the next morning. I was driven by the autonomy, the challenge, the purpose. I was intrinsically motivated.

To provide you a brief background, I created the company to help students with admissions to highly competitive graduate and professional programs. I believe everyone deserves access to higher education, notwithstanding racial, cultural, or socioeconomic status.

During this time, I realized something was not quite right with the admissions process. I could not understand how universities were accepting or rejecting applicants. Many seemingly excellent applicants were not getting accepted, while some students with multiple acceptances did not sincerely want to be there. Unbeknownst to me at the time, I was simply observing the impact of implicit bias against individuals from lower socioeconomic status and minority groups.

University admissions screening is incredibly challenging. How does one discern the few suitable applicants, amongst hundreds, thousands, or even tens of thousands, while being fair to everyone? How could one select students genuinely driven by the pursuit of the profession, rather than those primarily motivated by financial security, status, or social pressure?

Currently, most university admissions screening tools include the use of grades, personal statements, standardized testing, situational judgment tests, and interviews. The goal is always the same—to discern applicants based on academic acumen and people skills.

However, while searching for answers, I discovered no convincing scientific evidence to show that any of these practices could predict future on-the-job behavior. At best, they appeared to weakly correlate with future test performance. Even worse, was the fact that all these practices had been shown to cause profound bias against lower income individuals or individuals from minority groups.

Surprisingly, when I started to speak to admissions professionals, it seemed as if everybody knew the admissions process was not scientific—yet not everyone was motivated to initiate changes. Some argued they were being held back by bureaucracy, red tape, or the comfort of the status quo. Furthermore, others did not care, as a past University of Toronto president confided in me, because some admissions decision-makers simply liked to create "mini empires" and enjoyed "having control over young people's futures." In fact, he stated, these individuals were going to "fight tooth and nail" if anything threatened their control. While my jaw quite literally dropped and it took a while to push my eyebrows back into place from the back of my head, this clearly was not true for everyone—a vast majority of individuals I conferred with agreed that they are willing to try something new if it was fair and scientific. This is how I started on this journey.

BeMo quickly grew—from 1 founder to over 20 colleagues. It grew from helping a mere handful of students to helping thousands each year, and is currently still growing. We became the first and only company in education to offer full accountability to our students. I had established that we would only be in business if and only if we came up with scientifically-validated products and services and if we were confident they worked. To make our work even more difficult, we decided to offer a 100% satisfaction guarantee for all programs and an additional "get in or your money back" guarantee on a select few, to keep us on our toes at all times.

We did significantly better than I had anticipated. In the first year, we enjoyed a success rate of 83%; this gradually grew to a consistent success rate of over 90% for students who diligently followed our coaching programs.

The goals at BeMo were simple:

> To help alleviate the bias and barriers to access higher education, educating students on how to best present themselves and, more importantly, providing them with the essential skills to be better professionals, more responsible citizens, and, consequently, better future medical doctors, dentists, lawyers, or any other professional— essentially, all skills not taught in school, yet demanded during the admissions process. Students from higher socioeconomic status normally possess these skills; however, those from lower income families and minority groups may not. Unsurprisingly, this is a reason for implicit bias in traditional admissions screening practices (discussed in future chapters).

To learn more about admissions practices, since I did not know enough to offer my own admissions screening solution at the onset. I knew I had much to learn. I had to conduct my own experiments and dig into available literature, while helping students navigate the maze of professional school admissions, since most universities were unwilling to share any admissions information with us. For example, my attempts to gather more data from the University of Toronto and McMaster University were blocked by their "Freedom of Information" staff, citing the unavailability of records or trade secret restrictions, respectively. They even appeared to indicate their discontentment that I was "seeking information."

After 5 years at BeMo, helping students successfully prepare for various aspects of admissions—situational judgment tests, traditional interviews, and multiple mini interviews, combined with extensive literature research, interviewing admissions deans, and personal reflection—I was finally able to connect the dots.

This book is about what I learned from the traditional applicant screening practices, the vast literature on applicant selection, and, importantly, the literature in the field of psychology and the causes of human behaviors.

A word of warning: I am not holding back

I intend to put forth everything I have learned during my journey. This includes over 6 years of intense, deliberate work and over $200,000 dollars of my own money, spent on research and development. Some methods are new, some are borrowed from proven strategies of the past, some include a combination of old and new with a novel means to connect the dots.

If you are an admissions professional, I have vast admiration and respect for your impossible task. You have an incredible job, with enormous responsibility and even greater consequences.

In this book, I am going to tell it like it is, based on found facts. I am not holding back to be politically correct—I think being political is a betrayal of the self; no betrayal could be worse. A word of warning, some facts are going to offend closed minds, while delighting others who remain open-minded and are willing to try new strategies.

Furthermore, I acknowledge I do not know everything, not by any stretch of the imagination—a reason why I have delayed writing this book. Admissions screening is challenging. However, the fact that it could be difficult to know exactly how we should create a process that is effective, and fair does not mean there are no right or wrong ways of doing this. Rather, it simply implies that we have not yet discovered the best strategies and we need to continue the search. My goal is to contribute to moving forward in the right direction.

Your job is to judge the merits of each principle based on scientific facts and the willingness to experiment without the influence of ego, bureaucracy, or the unintended consequence of possibly offending a colleague or friend who disagrees without being privy to the same information. Of course, it also goes without saying that you should always adhere to the ethical and legal standards of your jurisdiction.

My hope is that after reading this book, you will be better able to select suitable applicants while simultaneously promoting diversity.

What you will learn

I believe applicant screening is more a science than an art—perhaps, this is my biased view on life, owed to my training as a scientist. I draw upon the fundamental laws in immunology (yes immunology!), psychology, sociology, evolutionary biology, statistics, physics, and chemistry. My goal is to provide a scientific view of applicant screening and selection, rather than an opinion piece. Notwithstanding, I have organized this book to include clear, real-life examples to make the connections obvious, rather than writing a dry scientific review.

First, I intend to outline a scientific view on why diversity is of the utmost importance and how to promote diversity during the university admissions process. I emphasize "scientific" so as not to confuse the term diversity with a political tool, often over-used yet seldom implemented by our politicians.

After our discussion about the importance of diversity, I shall provide a historical overview of the applicant screening process, reviewing fundamental problems with traditional practices. This section will take us back to the invention of standardization in education and discuss the pitfalls of using personal statements, grades, standardized tests, situational judgment tests, and various formats of in-person interviews. Specifically, we will witness the inability of these practices to predict future on-the-job behavior and their susceptibility to cause profound bias against lower income and minority applicants. Thereafter, I will review the dire consequences of using traditional applicant screening practices and define what would classify as a "good" admissions screening process.

Subsequently, I offer 14 specific "Rules" to select top-performing applicants while promoting diversity. Again, I will define each rule, providing specific examples and any experimental evidence behind each principle.

This is to be followed by a discussion on how to democratize our educational systems and admissions screening process, based on the foundations of democracy in this modern world. I view this as essential to stimulate positive change in our education system and to allow for continuous innovation.

I will conclude by providing a specific framework on how to design questions based on the 14 Rules to detect the essential Big Three characteristics to be assessed in applicants. Moreover, I will offer a list of sample questions and indicate how to discern suitable applicants based on the type of answers provided.

Why promoting diversity is essential, as proven by science

> *"Strength lies in differences, not in similarities."*
> —Stephen R. Covey

I believe the best laws are the ones that have stood the test of time—the ones that have been tested over and over and are thus the laws of nature. One of these, is that of natural selection, which in evolutionary biology is when nature selects traits most favorable in specific environments, allowing certain organisms to flourish and others to perish overtime. This is accomplished through genetic diversity and essential for populations to adapt to changing environments. Over time, it results in the presence of increasingly diverse traits and/or species in various environments. For example, there are an estimated 9 million species on Earth; this is a continuously growing number. Each of these species play an important role in their ecosystem, impacting others either directly or indirectly. This undeniable connectivity and reliance of different species on each other for survival is a clear indication that diversity is essential and is why nature continues to push for greater diversity.

The same law applies to human populations. Having populations of diverse groups of individuals with diverse genetics, traits, personalities, and points of views can allow a population to adapt to changing environments and challenges more effectively. Different individuals have different strengths; collectively, as a group, we have been able to accomplish some remarkable feats collaborating with individuals of varying strengths and weaknesses. Furthermore, there exists evidence that smaller human populations with less diverse genetics, due to inbreeding, suffer significantly higher rates of the late onset of complex diseases, such as coronary heart disease, stroke, cancer, uni/bipolar depression, asthma, gout, and peptic ulcer.[1]

Additionally, the disadvantages of reduced diversity impact the intellectual capacity of organizations. Those with individuals very similar in their behavior and thinking are less adaptive to new challenges, failing to consider or encourage different perspectives, seeing things mostly in black and white and, consequently, suffering from groupthink fallacy. A classic example is the study of deleterious effects of groupthink in an organization setting of Swissair.[2] Founded in 1931, Swissair was at a time so successful, it was called "the Flying Bank." Over time, the management came to the false belief that the company was infallible and superior to its competitors. Furthermore, they reorganized the company to create a homogeneous group, leading to the loss of expertise and opposing views required for continued innovation, culminating with the company's eventual demise in 2002.

Since Swissair, the impact of diversity on organizations has been extensively studied. Richard Freeman and Wei Huang found, in a study of more than 2.5 million academic publications, that papers with more diverse authors have higher impact factors and are cited more often.[3] A study on price bubbles in markets reported that diverse markets of traders are 58% more likely to value market prices accurately compared to homogeneous markets.[4] A publication by Samuel R. Sommers, indicated that diverse groups of juries in mock trials, outperformed decision making of all-White juries by deliberating longer and raising more facts.[5]

It is thus clear that populations with a greater level of diversity are better able to solve problems and innovate over time, as compared to ones that are isolated and homogenous. For this reason, one's goal as an admissions dean, director, or officer must be to promote diversity. After all, your accepted applicants are to be your source for fresh ideas, not just during their training but later, as colleagues, faculty members, and alumni.

Promoting diversity

The question now is how to promote diversity while being fair to all applicants. Three basic methods that come to mind include the following.

1) To arbitrarily increase the level of enrollment for underrepresented minority groups, guaranteeing them several seats per entering class. This is easy to implement (for example, affirmative action in the United States or similar policies for indigenous populations in Canada and elsewhere).

2) To create a merit-based, scientific admissions process without implicit bias based on gender or racial, cultural, and socioeconomic background. This method has eluded most to date and is thus the most challenging consideration; it is the main topic of discussion here.

3) A combination of both considerations above.

The problems with approaches similar to the first point (and as a result, the third) are that while they try to promote diversity, they actually explicitly discriminate against majority groups, rejecting majority applicants that score higher in the admissions process to make room for underrepresented minorities. This practice is an indirect admittance by educational institutions that their current practices introduce racial, cultural, and socioeconomic bias; therefore, in order to level the playing field, it is best to reserve some spots for underrepresented groups.

The flaw in this approach is obvious. Our approach should be to first use practices that do not introduce bias, rather than insist on using ineffective practices and trying to remedy the problem by introducing other problematic "solutions" that create further bias and discrimination, based on race, ethnicity, or economics. In fact, this practice has resulted in contentious lawsuits against several universities in the US—for example, in 2014, against Harvard by Asian-Americans. The lawsuit, led by activist Edward Blum, alleged that Harvard discriminated against Asian-Americans with higher scores to make room for minority applicants having scored lower on average. Regardless of its resolution, this problem persists.

The other problem with this approach is that often, while a certain number of seats might be "guaranteed" for certain minority groups, such applicants are continued to be assessed using traditional applicant screening practices, causing a significant implicit bias against them as we will witness shortly in the next chapter. For example, as of writing this book, McMaster University medical school indicates the following policy on its website about indigenous applicants wishing to pursue medicine: "Indigenous applicants are required to complete the OMSAS application and must meet the <u>same minimum academic criteria for admission as set out for the general pool of candidates</u> (three or more years of undergraduate degree-level courses by May of the year of entry with an overall GPA of at least 3.00 as calculated on the OMSAS 4.00 scale and a minimum score of 6 on the Verbal Reasoning component of the MCAT or 123 on the Critical

Analysis and Reasoning section of the MCAT 2015 and CASPer)."

Alternately, the second approach ensures that the process is fair, transparent, and meritocratic, selecting students based on indicators of future behavior that do not correlate with socioeconomic status, race, gender, or cultural background. In my opinion, this is the best way to select top-performing future professionals while promoting diversity.

I take my own medicine

Before diving into specific strategies, I would like to make clear that this book is not about an untested theory or a literature review. All discussed considerations have been personally tested in my two businesses, with my own money and livelihood on the line. I do take my own medicine on a regular basis. This allows me to continuously test and refine my protocols. It forces me to ensure what we offer works and has real value in life.

This is in stark contrast to most other available admissions screening tools, since those are not used in this manner. For example, an admissions test introduced by a Canadian public university, and later turned into a spin off company that provides situational judgment tests, does not appear to be currently used by the university or the company to hire their own staff as of writing this book. None of the founders, university admissions staff, or any employees have been selected using the same tool that they continuously want the world to adopt. Of course, it is alarming that individuals and organizations who preach the use of a new screening tool are not willing to use it themselves. If the screening tool is as good as they claim, wouldn't it make sense for them to use it on their own job applicants?

Moreover, I decided early on not to collaborate with any universities to develop our software and systems because I believe universities should remain a hub for continuous research. In my opinion, educational institutions that commit to creating spin-off for-profit companies from their own research, create an impediment to growth and progress. One can argue that, under such circumstances, they would be less willing to adopt new and better ideas or technologies that would threaten the existence of their for-profit companies. This is especially true in the field of admissions screening, because such practices usually cause a disservice for the public due to clear conflict of interest of the host university and its spin-off company. On the other hand, university independent initiatives are constantly field tested and because of continuous competition with other companies, most companies are forced to constantly improve their products and services to survive.

As a result, I was forced to find other ways to test my new strategies and develop them based on my literature research and personal experiments. I have tested these principles during my own hiring practices and by conducting experiments to test new questions with the help of students who we train for traditional admissions tests at BeMo. I screen, on average, about 100 applicants per month for various jobs at BeMo and SortSmart; we help a significantly greater number of students at BeMo, which has provided me a fantastic opportunity to test everything on a large, highly diverse population.

Initially, I was unable to hire any full-time employees to last over 6 months; however, that number has changed quickly to over 3 years after our screening process was optimized.

The results since have been remarkable! In fact, I believe our competitive advantage has been the ability to select top performers genuinely as interested as myself in the pursuit of our vision while promoting diversity. At times, we joke our team is like the United Nations General Assembly. Its members are from various racial, cultural, and socioeconomic backgrounds, with an almost even gender distribution, which tilts slightly toward females.

We are now ready to dive deep into these strategies, starting with what one must avoid first. I am intentionally starting with such problematic practices—not only do they provide the quickest way to transform any admissions screening process when avoided, but some are so toxic, they should be shunned at all costs or, better yet, completely banned.

Go to AdmissionsHealthCalculator.com to calculate the health of your admissions screening process in less than ten seconds.

Chapter II

Top 6 Admissions Screening Practices to Avoid

"The important thing to do is to never stop questioning."
—Albert Einstein

#1. The problems with grades and standardized test scores

The use of standardized testing and grade point average (GPA), which do not appear to serve a scientific basis for selection, ironically originate from the work of 3 prominent figures in the scientific community, dating back to the 1800s. They were disparagingly referred to as "averagerians" by British poet William

Cyples[6]—a term presently employed by an individuality expert at Harvard, Professor Todd Rose, in his book *The End of Average*. The historical facts presented in this fascinating book merit discussion here in the context of admissions screening.

Adolphe Quetelet, born in 1796, started his career as an astronomer. At the peak of his career, he was appointed director of Belgium's observatory, which he had helped establish. At this time, astronomers realized the significant variability in calculations regarding the speed of celestial objects by different astronomers. The then solution was the use of what is today known as the "method of averages"— combining all known measurements into an average. Some members of the community advocated this method was more accurate than any single measurement.[7,8] In 1830, as Belgium rushed into the chaos of revolution, Quetelet's career was disrupted. This event inspired him to find a scientific method to manage society. His primary solution was to use the method of averages for social problems and people, advocating that the individual represented the error and that average measurements were more of an accurate indication of the true value of any measurement.[9] Quetelet went on to create a vast array of averages as a point of reference. He created the average chest circumference of Scottish soldiers,[10] average stature, average weight, average number of people in poverty, average amount of education, and the average age of death. In fact, he invented the earlier version of the "body mass index" (BMI), originally called the Quetelet Index, to establish average health. To Quetelet, "if an individual at any given epoch of society possessed all the qualities of the Average Man, he would represent all that is great, good, or beautiful,"[11] while any deviations "would constitute Monstrosity."[12] This propelled Quetelet into stardom as a genius of his time, celebrated by notable scientists and scholars—from Karl Marx to James Maxwell, and many others.[13-16]

Quetelet's works were admired and continued by the prominent British mathematician Sir Francis Galton, who eventually became one of Quetelet's critics.[17] While Quetelet believed that the ideal individuals were those closer to the average and deviations from the average represented "errors," Galton claimed the average to be far from the ideal and rather mediocre.[18] Galton, concerned by the declining rate of innovation of the British empire, believed anything above average was closer to the ideal and thus desirable, while anything below average was undesirable. Furthermore, he believed that desirable traits were correlated with each other, such that someone who was educated or wealthy was more likely to be better off than average in regards to health, beauty, and intelligence.[19,20] As a member of the wealthy upper class himself, his solution to declining British innovation was to rank people according to their relative position to the average class.[21] He believed the best way to advance civilization was to improve upon the average, stating, "what nature does blindly, slowly, and ruthlessly, man may do providently, quickly, and kindly."[21] He went on to create 14 different classes for members of society, ranking individuals from "Imbeciles" (the lowest rank), to "Mediocre" (the middle rank), to "Eminent" (the highest rank).[22]

While Quetelet and Galton championed average-erianism, it was Fredrick Winslow Taylor and Edward Thorndike who standardized businesses and education, respectively.

Taylor, born in 1856, to a wealthy, upper-class family from Pennsylvania, spent 2 years studying in Prussia, which was fully organized using Quetelet's ideas.[23] On his return to Pennsylvania, Taylor decided to work in 2 factories owned by family friends—he saw an opportunity to organize the factories around the concept of standardization for better efficiency during the Industrial Revolution. First, he worked at Enterprise Hydraulic Works and later, at Midvale Steelwork, where he was quickly promoted to the role of chief engineer.[24,25]

Taylor believed that "an organization composed of individuals of mediocre ability, working in accordance with policies, plans, and procedures discovered by analysis of the fundamental facts of their situation, in the long run prove more successful and stable than an organization of geniuses, each led by inspiration."[26] He thus sought to standardize all aspects of factory work, creating standardized operation procedures for each task. The workers were to be trained to perform these task exactly as ordered by their "managers," a new role created at the time that we all take for granted today.[27-30]

As factories expanded during the Industrial Revolution, a clear need for high school-educated workers continued to grow at an exponential rate. This came at a time when only 6% of the American population had graduated from high school and only 2% had graduated from college.[31] To satisfy needs, schools around the United States adopted Taylorism tenets of "scientific management" to standardize education, to create students good enough to be able to work at the factories. This was around the same time when school bells were introduced to mimic factory bells and condition students for their future factory jobs.[32-33] In essence, as H. L. Mencken, an American journalist at the time, mentioned, the aim of the education system was to "reduce as many individuals as possible to the same safe level," and "to put down dissent and originality."[34]

Edward Lee Thorndike, a most prominent educational psychologist,[35] assessed Taylor's ideas with a twist, similar to Galton's adoption of Quetelet's ideas of the average man. He believed the role of standardization in education was to rank students as superior, mediocre, and inferior; he declared that "quality is more important than equality." Similar to Galton, he believed if students were good in a particular area, such as achieving high scores in high school, they were more likely to do better in college and later on in life, in whatever they wished to pursue. Furthermore, he believed that mental capacity was established at birth, not with education. Accordingly, superior students were to be showered with support to attend college and in later leadership roles. Mediocre students were to be readied and sent to factory jobs; inferior and slow-learning students would be offered additional support to save resources.[36–37]

But how were schools to rank students? Thorndike's answer was through using standardized tests. He created these tests for many aspects of education, including arithmetic, reading, and comprehension. He created entrance exams for colleges, even creating one for law school. He believed that the best way to rank students was using GPA and standardized test scores—colleges should only admit students with the best scores.[38]

Fundamental errors in selection based on grades and standardized test scores

The first problem that should be obvious in hindsight from Thorndike's thinking is assuming an individual with high standardized test scores and GPA, or the ability to do well on such tests, is more likely to be successful later in real life and, as a result, more likely to become a better doctor, lawyer, pharmacist, or any other professional.

This is flawed thinking: it assumes, without empirical proof, a 100% correlation between the ability to do well on standardized testing, achieving good grades and the ability to do many other things to become a successful future professional. Even more short-sighted was the belief that all mental capabilities were correlated. For example, James Cattel, a proponent of Galton, conducted a series of experiments in the 1890s at Columbia University looking for correlations between a series of mental tests, hoping to find a strong correlation. However, Cattell found no correlation between any of the tests, such as the ability to name colors and the ability to judge when a certain amount of time had elapsed. Furthermore, he found weak correlation between students' college grades and any of these mental tests.[39] Surprisingly, even Thorndike's experiments showed weak correlation between grades, standardized test scores, and future on-the-job success; yet, he had clearly ignored the results of his own findings.[40]

Test validity and correlation

The previous section allows us to safely conclude that grades and standardized tests during Thorndike's time were not a valid measure of future success. They are no better indicators of future performance today either; but, before I provide specific examples, let's discuss validity.

What is test validity? Test validity is the ability of a test to actually measure the construct it is designed to measure. For example, a thermometer is a valid tool for measuring the temperature of a room yet it is not a valid tool for measuring the distance between 2 points in space.

Another important aspect of test validity is the correlation between the test and the construct it is designed to measure. The stronger the correlation, the better predictive value a test has. Correlation coefficient (r) is expressed as a number between 0 and 1, where 0 indicates no correlation, such as the chances of winning the lottery and having blue eyes, and 1 shows a perfect correlation, such as temperature of a room in Celsius versus in Fahrenheit. Furthermore, the r value to the power of 2 multiplied by 100 provides the percentage the variation in one variable is correlated with the variation in another. For example, if the correlation coefficient for 2 variables is 0.7, it means that 49% of the variance is related. Another fact is the completely arbitrary set of rules that determine what is considered "strong" versus "weak" correlation. In most fields, a correlation coefficient of 0.8 or higher is considered a "strong" correlation, while 0.4 or lower is considered "weak." Anything between 0.4 and 0.8 is considered "moderate." However, this is entirely arbitrary. Even at an r value of 0.7, we can explain less than half (49%) of the relatedness of 2 variables. For example, imagine being operated on by a brain surgeon who had only completed half their training and was only able to operate successfully less than half of the time! I hope this allows you to view correlational studies with a more critical eye, which brings me to the correlation of grades/GPA and standardized tests with real-life performance in our modern world.

Let us consider the Scholastic Assessment Test (SAT), the Medical College Admissions Test (MCAT), and Grade Point Average (GPA). The correlation between SAT scores and the first-semester of undergraduate studies was found to be a mere 0.4.[41] The correlation between MCAT scores and future performance were also found to be weak, both in terms of future U.S. Medical Licensure Exam (USMLE) performance and other residency performance assessments.[42] Specifically, in a study, the authors found weak correlation between MCAT scores and USMLE scores ranging from Cramér's V values of 0.05 to 0.24, which is similar to an r value, but involves the correlation between two nominal variables.[42] In another study, the authors showed that the MCAT was *not* able to predict actual on-the-job performance based on residency program director assessment.[43] As for the GPA? In yet another study, the authors showed that medical school GPA showed a weak correlation to future performance as junior doctors with an r value of 0.23.[44]

Let us review that again. The data shows that SAT is not able to predict undergraduates' academic performance. The MCAT cannot predict USMLE performance or on-the-job performance. GPA cannot predict performance of junior doctors. Similar findings have been found in all other professions, using other formats of standardized testing; yet, we see many continue to insist on using such practices to sort through applicants.

First, almost all these correlations are really weak at explaining any relationship between the variables, even by arbitrary standards of correlational studies. Notably, there's a fundamental error of judgment. It is as if we have been asking the wrong questions—Do we really care about a test that is able to predict future tests? Or do we care about the correlation between a test and the actual real-life job performance in the future? You would probably agree that the latter makes more sense. Grades and standardized tests can only tell us (barely and if at all), whether a student is likely to do well on similar future tests; but, the reality is that they cannot tell us how the person is going to behave in real-life situations because real life does not include standardized tests and report cards.

Ultimately, it is no wonder that these Thorndike practices do not work in today's world. A lot has changed since the early 1900s. Imagine if we insisted on using horses and buggies for transportation or snail mail for communication to this date.

Even worse, neither grades nor standardized test scores can tell us about the motivation of the applicants. Additionally, they appear to cause bias against applicants from lower income levels or those belonging to minority groups[45-48] prompting several prominent schools, such as the University of Chicago to drop their standardized testing requirements.

#2 The problems with personal statements and list of experiences

The personal statement or any form of list of past experiences is another common selection tool for many schools and programs. However, few studies exist, if any, demonstrating their effectiveness as a selection tool. In an assessment of the selection for health care professions, Prideaux et al. found no evidence that these are reliable or that they have any predictive validity.[49] In another review of personal qualities in selection, Albanese et al. found no evidence that the personal statement measured anything different than the interview.[50] Furthermore, Wouters et al. found that one cannot distinguish between selected and non-selected applicants on the basis of written statements on motivation.[51]

The unreliability of personal or autobiographical statements is not difficult to reason. Applicants have almost unlimited time in which to craft their statement. It is extremely difficult to verify the veracity of personal history statements. There are countless guides, workshops, and classes on how to compose the "ideal" statement, resulting in a homogeneity of work. Personal history and background information betray the anonymity of the process (if one is indeed imposed); the applicant can then become vulnerable to implicit biases of the audience. One can argue that wealthy applicants have even more time to perfect their personal statements, because they are not required to work full-time (or even part-time), which provides them with more time to complete such applications. Notwithstanding, wealthy applicants also have access to better resources for help.

Personal and autobiographical statements are not more useful than perfunctory tasks; they may be harmful to the selection process. Combine this with the time and resources required to sort through thousands of personal statements; now, you have a completely futile system for applicant selection.

#3. The problems with situational judgment tests

The use of web-based situational judgment tests is an attempt towards a more scientifically rational approach to candidate selection. A handful of private companies are offering such services, attempting to bring in a truly outdated technology, which has been used by businesses for decades, as a novel "solution." For example, in one such test, candidates are shown hypothetical, real-life situations in a video or written prompt and asked how they would respond. The test is claimed to examine "non-cognitive" abilities, such as problem solving, decision-making, and interpersonal skills. Essentially, the reviewers judge whether an applicant responds "appropriately" in a given situation. While these tests purport to be more reliable as a selection tool, they too have significant shortcomings.

Asking hypothetical questions generally leads applicants to provide socially acceptable responses. This can be best explained by the "context principle"—our behaviors are modified by the context of our environment.[52] Therefore, asking someone in a test setting how they would react to some hypothetical situation might not be of any value, since the person knows they are being tested and that their response has to be one that brings on a favorable outcome, such as being accepted to their program of choice. This means that the person might not necessarily act in the same way under real-life situations without supervision and test pressures. This is the same reason why it is not possible to label anyone with any personality trait. For example, someone who may be shy in one setting—such as a child in the presence of adults—might be overly outgoing in another setting—the same child with her friends.

Judging whether a response to a delicate or stressful, imagined scenario is appropriate can vary across cultures. These tests are singularly guided by accepted Western cultural norms. This can pose significant challenges to non-native applicants or those immersed in another culture. The diverse cultural identity of the United States, the United Kingdom, and Canada, for example, implies this is a significant issue for applicants. At the 2016 medical education conference in Canada, the New York Medical College (NYMC) reported that underrepresented minority applicants scored lower on such a situational judgment test—Computer-based Assessment for Sampling Personal Characteristics ("CASPer")—as compared to other applicants, and males scored lower than females, thus creating a gender bias.[72] Related to this is a caveat in all tests that claim to test "non-cognitive" skills—the applicant provides the answer they think the reviewers want to hear. Applicants from more advantaged socioeconomic backgrounds, on average, have stronger cognitive and non-cognitive skills than those from lower socioeconomic strata, owed to their economically-biased childhood experiences. Situational judgment tests may discriminate against socio-economically disadvantaged applicants who had lacked the opportunity to develop or refine their non-cognitive skills as a result of their lesser social, economic, and cultural capital. Moreover, such tests add yet another barrier to lower income applicants—adding further costs to the already costly application process and tuition for selected applicants.

Additionally, such tests assume that people are born with certain personal and professional characteristics—similar to Thorndike—by claiming that they are "immune" to test preparation. This is not only fundamentally incorrect but given that all personal and professional behaviors are learned behavior, it is a dangerous claim that can amount to discrimination. Empirical evidence has repeatedly shown that personality traits are at best only 40–50% heritable and continue to develop with age, indicating that they are mostly formed as a result of interactions with one's environment.[53]

Situational judgment tests do not appear to have been validated to correlate with actual on-the-job behavior; the best correlation found appears to have been self-reported by the creators of the for-profit spin-off company from McMaster University selling such products. In their pilot study, the authors reported a low correlation of r = 0.3–0.5 between the computer-based situational judgment test (CASPer) and the multiple mini interview (MMI) another format of assessment created by some of the same authors at McMaster, and test scores in future medical licensing examinations.[54,55] First, in my opinion, the study suffers from the law of small numbers and confidence over doubt bias,[56] due to small sample sizes and the conflict of interest between the authors and the host university. It is not generally possible to make a broad conclusion about the reliability and validity of any assessment tool using a sample population of 110 to 167 as reported in the study.[54] Furthermore, all participants were selected from a pool of applicants to McMaster's medical school, rather than a random population.[54] Second, note that the test is merely a predictor of future test performance; and the correlation is weak at best and able to explain up to a maximum of 25% of the variance between the 2 variables.[54]

To make matters worse, situational judgment tests appear to be highly coachable, being systematically designed and scored—it is thus easy for applicants to learn to predictably provide an acceptable response. In fact, given the evidence that situational judgment tests appear to cause bias, a mission at BeMo was to ensure no one was treated unfairly due to the use of situational judgment tests; this lead us to create a preparation program for 2 situational judgment tests used by some schools—namely CASPer and MMI. Our preparation programs have been shown to increase applicants' practice scores by 23–27%, for both CASPer and MMI, respectively (Figure 1). In this study, a random pool of 24 applicants for CASPer and another pool of 44 applicants for MMI were coached for each test. First, the applicants' baseline scores were determined using a realistic mock test and then the applicants were coached using additional independent simulations followed by coaching to highlight areas of improvement. This process was continued for 3 sessions for CASPer and between 6 to 8 sessions for MMI. The results demonstrate that applicants' practice scores significantly increased following preparation in both of these independent studies. Of note, both the applicants and the coaches were unaware of the study to avoid confounding variables. While the sample sizes were small, this is remarkably significant, not only statistically, but in absolute terms, since coaching intervention in educational programs has been shown to cause a minor change of about 5–10% in most cases. Furthermore, by extrapolation one can argue that coaching will have similar results on actual test scores.

CASPer & MMI Practice Scores Before and After Coaching Intervention

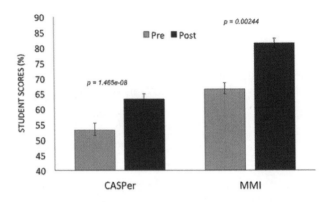

Figure 1. Coaching intervention significantly increases applicants' CASPer and MMI practice scores by 23 and 27% respectively.

Lastly, situational judgment tests do not appear to measure the level of intrinsic motivation of each applicant (Figure 2). This is important to note and we will discuss this in detail in Rule 2 because intrinsic motivation is the desire to engage in an activity that is found to be rewarding on its own without the need for any external rewards or punishments and is the best predictor of future behavior based on over 40 years of research.

**Motivation of Medical School Students and Residents
Selected Using Different Admissions Interviews
Formats & Situational Judgment Tests**

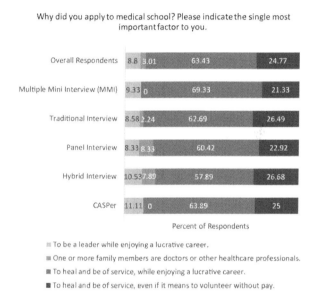

Why did you apply to medical school? Please indicate the single most important factor to you.

Overall Respondents	8.8	3.01	63.43	24.77
Multiple Mini Interview (MMI)	9.33	0	69.33	21.33
Traditional Interview	8.58	2.24	62.69	26.49
Panel Interview	8.33	8.33	60.42	22.92
Hybrid Interview	10.53	7.89	57.89	26.68
CASPer	11.11	0	63.89	25

Percent of Respondents

▨ To be a leader while enjoying a lucrative career.
▩ One or more family members are doctors or other healthcare professionals.
▤ To heal and be of service, while enjoying a lucrative career.
▪ To heal and be of service, even if it means to volunteer without pay.

Figure 2. 75% of medical school students and residents indicate that the primary reason for pursuing a career in medicine is due to extrinsic factors such as wealth, status, or familial pressure regardless of the admissions screening tool used to select them.

#4. The problems with in-person interviews

The problems with most interviews are similar to those we recently discussed for situational judgment tests. For example, interviews are not a valid measure of predicting future on-the-job performance because of the context principle. Furthermore, the context principle provides an edge to students coming from higher socioeconomic backgrounds, since they are better able to anticipate socially acceptable responses. Moreover, in-person interviews add yet another barrier for lower income-background students, owed to costs associated with traveling to other cities for the interviews. Notably, interviews fail to detect applicants' intrinsic motivation. There is arguably more damage done during the interview stage than in other stages.

The interview, face-to-face contact with a single, a series, or a panel of interviewers with varying degrees of structure, are common parts of the selection processes. The interview step for most applications follows an initial narrowing down of the applicant pool using grades, standardized admissions test scores, personal statements, and/or situational judgment tests. This implies that not all students will have an opportunity to personally meet with an interviewer. Therefore, by the time students make it to the in-person interview stage, the errors made with such practices are already amplified. Interviews are costly and difficult logistical operations for an institution, requiring the management of time for the applicants/interviewers and the use of appropriate locations, to list a few. These investments may be justified if the in-person interview was a reliable method for selecting applicants. Unfortunately, studies have shown that the interview is not a robust selection measure.[57]

The reason behind the lack of reliability of this method is seemingly obvious and determined solely by the reliability of the person conducting the interview. A study by Quintero et al. illustrates this well.[58] In a study of 135 interviewers, it was found that some gave candidates more favorable rankings when personality preferences matched, as measured by the Myers–Briggs scale. Unsurprisingly, interviewers are subconsciously drawn to applicants most like themselves. The result of relying on this selection criterion will ensure that the future classes of professional schools resemble those of the past, thus progressively reducing diversity.

The development of more recent interview approaches (such as a series of mini interviews or MMIs) try to remedy this issue, using multiple raters or reviewers. I tend to agree with MMI (and CASPer) creators that using multiple independent raters should theoretically lead to more reliable assessment tools. While the MMI is claimed to be reliable and reported to correlate with the performance on future tests by their creators[59-61], independent research has highlighted several problems. Their reliability appears to fluctuate in different settings,[62-65] their administration is costly,[66-67] and they require more reviewers, standardized parameters, and careful coordination. Moreover, developers must assume that all items included in any particular test version be fully exposed. Furthermore, given their complex and costly nature, it is not feasible to administer mini interviews for the entire applicant pool, resulting in further bias and unfairness, and, importantly, the possibility of missing well-suited applicants arbitrary filtered out at the initial stages using GPA, standardized tests, personal statements, and/or situational judgment tests. For example, as of writing this book, McMaster University warns applicants on its admissions website that "Due to the nature of the Multiple Mini-Interview, video-conference or telephone interviews are not possible."

Most notably, the MMI has been found to introduce bias against lower income individuals, underrepresented minority groups,[68-69] and male applicants,[70] similar to what has been reported by NYMC about CASPer.[62] MMIs also appears to put introverted applicants at a disadvantage.[73]

The inconsistency about MMIs and, particularly, its impact on disadvantaged applicants,[74] prompted its creators to write an opinion piece as an invited commentary, where they appeared to suggest contradictory results are due to variations across institutions and not because there exist flaws in the MMIs.[75] The authors argued that "rather than suggesting that the inconsistent and at times contrary results of MMI studies should repudiate the MMI's value... What if *all* of the studies are right?"[75]

This is a curious conclusion, to say the least, due to the definition of a scientific theory, and perhaps unsurprising given the conflict of interest for at least one of the authors, a director of the company that seemingly provides MMIs as a for-profit product. A theory normally remains a hypothesis. It can never be proven; no matter how many correct observations are made. However, a single observation that contradicts the prediction of a hypothesis will disprove a theory. There have been several observations that contradict the predictions of usefulness of MMIs to date. Furthermore, if such a reasoning by the authors is accurate, then one might expect that McMaster University's admissions practices—as the creator of the MMI and as host to the authors—should not indicate any form of bias.

To test the MMI creators' assertion, we compared the results of 3 independent studies of medical school students and residents conducted in the United States and Canada. The first 2 confirmed the presence of bias against lower income individuals; the observed bias did not differ based on the admissions selection tool used to select applicants during the admissions process, including the use of MMIs or CASPer (Figure 3).

Family Income Distribution of Medical School Students and Residents Selected Using Different Admissions Interviews Formats & Situational Judgment Tests

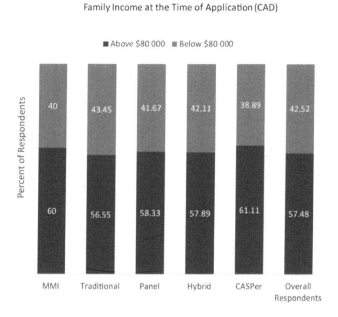

Family Income at the Time of Application (CAD)

■ Above $80 000   ■ Below $80 000

Figure 3. Accepted medical school applicants from higher income families are the most represented group regardless of the admissions screening tool used to select them.

In the third study, we focused on applicants accepted to McMaster University medical school versus those accepted to any of the other medical schools in Canada. Results showed that McMaster University's admissions practices do not appear to be significantly different from others' in terms of implicit bias, regardless of the use of MMIs or CASPer (Figure 4 & 5).

**Family Income and Racial Profile of Medical School
Students and Residents Accepted to McMaster Medical
School in Comparison to Those Accepted to Other
Canadian Medical Schools**

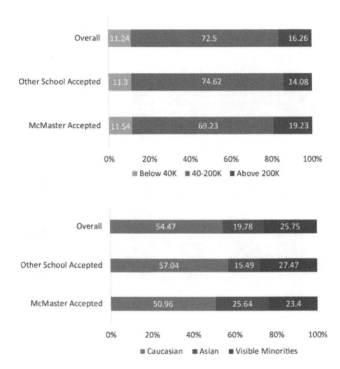

Figure 4. Family income distribution (top) and racial profile
(bottom) of medical school applicants accepted to McMaster
University is not significantly different from those accepted to other
Canadian medical schools.

Family Income Distribution of Medical School Students and Residents Selected with or without the Use of CASPer or MMI

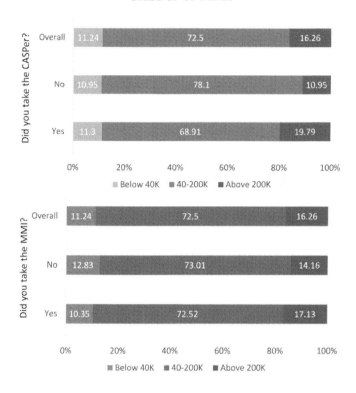

Figure 5. Family income distribution of accepted medical school applicants using CASPer (top) or MMI (bottom) is not significantly different from those accepted without the use of such admissions screening tools.

I will shortly review the details of the studies in the subsection titled "The consequences of continuing to use outdated admissions screening practices."

#5. The problems with letters of recommendation

Like the personal statement, this measure is both common and ineffective. There exists no empirical evidence supporting the reliability of letters of reference in the selection process. The applicant can unfairly affect the process by simply selecting their best references (usually 3); however, it is difficult to verify the veracity of each letter for the entire applicant pool, if not impossible. That means that just like in the interview stage, most reference letters are not even considered until a significant proportion of the entire applicant pool has been screened out. This fact alone makes reference letters both unfair and unscientific.

But there is more. If the applicant has good and bad work experiences, asking for a very small sample will not provide an adequate assessment of that applicant. Another issue with letters of reference is of opportunity and accessibility, both of which may depend on one's socioeconomic status. Access to influential and established professionals within a field and a reference letter from the same can put an applicant at a significant advantage. However, this advantage comes from the strength of the referee rather than the strengths of the applicant. It can also introduce professional politics into the selection process; these, again, are indicative of the referee and their professional standing, rather than of the applicant's merit.

#6. The problems with using "rolling admissions"

Rolling admissions are the policy of accepting applications over an extended period of time; however, offering acceptance letters on a rolling basis is also problematic. First, due to primacy effect, the first batch of applicants always seem more attractive, leading to most spots being filled quickly without equal consideration given to applications received later during the admissions cycle. Second, this policy normally favors the wealthy, since they have more time and are able to put together a stellar application much sooner, as compared to students who may have to work part-time or full-time in addition to attending school. Third, it is unfathomable how one can possibly choose the best applicants from the entire pool if all applicants are not evaluated before a decision is made.

As we just observed, grades, standardized admissions tests, personal statements, situational judgment tests, interviews, reference letters, and rolling admissions do not predict anything valuable or, worse, cause profound bias. Therefore, the fundamental question is this: Why are we still using these practices as a means to screen applicants? You probably agree now that while these methods might have been the best during the Industrial Revolution and may have done a lot of good for our society at the time, they are no longer valid methods of assessment for selecting the best-suited applicants. Their continued use can have dire consequences.

The consequences of continued use of outdated screening practices

Having addressed the pitfalls of using traditional admissions screening protocols, I would like to now share their real-life consequences, based on our research at SortSmart and those conducted by other groups, including published data by the official governing bodies.

There exist many reports indicating that, on average, students admitted to professional schools are significantly wealthier, as compared to the general population, and that minority groups are underrepresented.[76-78]

To pinpoint the cause for the observed bias, we recently conducted 2 independent studies of the medical school admissions process in the United States and Canada, anonymously surveying random samples of 469 and 452 medical students and residents in each country, respectively.

The results pointed to several important findings, including the lack of intrinsic motivation by the majority of accepted applicants, wealth bias compared to the general population, and a notable lack of trust in the current admissions practices. I will emphasize the last point again. *Even applicants who fared well and were accepted voiced concerns about the admissions process!*

I would like to point out that our sample populations appear to be representative because the reported demographic are within +/-5% of those reported by the American Association of Medical Colleges (AAMC) and the Association of Faculties of Medicine of Canada (AFMC). I will summarize the main findings below from our US study, but I have included a link to the full study details at the end of this section, including the methodology, study validation, a TEDx talk, and a presentation of the study results at the Beyond Sciences Initiative International Conference, for those interested to learn more. Note, the observed trends in Canada (Table 1), which uses the same admissions screening practices as the United States, are almost identical. This is interesting because the same practices have indicated similar patterns in 2 distinct geographical locations; this provides further evidence that the bias is due to the admissions practices used and likely not as a result of other possible cofounding factors.

Summary of Findings in 2 Independent Survey Studies of Medical School Students and Residents in the United States and Canada

	United States	Canada
Sample Size	469	452
Margin of Error	+/- 5%	+/- 5%
Intrinsically Motivated	25%	32%
Willing to Advocate for a New and Improved Admissions Process	94%	97%
Accepted Applicants from Families with Over $100K/Year Income	36%	37%
Percentage of Caucasians from Families with Over $100K/Year Income	69%	64%
Percentage of Visible Minorities from Families with Below $80K/Year Income	61%	64%

Table 1. Highlights of findings from 2 independent survey studies of medical school students and resident from the United States and Canada.

The results reveal 3 fundamental findings:

First, the survey showed that even successful applicants (medical students and residents) did not have full confidence in the current admissions practices. Specifically, 90–95% of all respondents believe that the current admissions practices are not the best means to select applicants; 94–97% indicated their willingness to support a new, improved, and transparent admissions screening tool (Figure 6).

Opinion of Medical School Students and Residents about Current Admissions Screening Tool

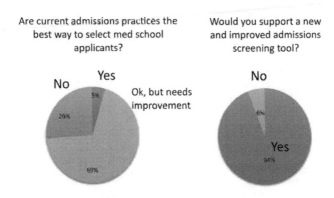

Figure 6. 95% of medical school students and residents indicate that current admissions practices require improvement with 94% indicating willingness to support a new and improved and transparent admissions screening tool.

Second, the survey showed that medical school admissions processes appear to favor applicants from higher income families—respondents from higher income families were consistently overrepresented, as compared to the general population (Figure 7).

Family Income Distribution of Medical School Students and Residents at the Time of Application to Medical School

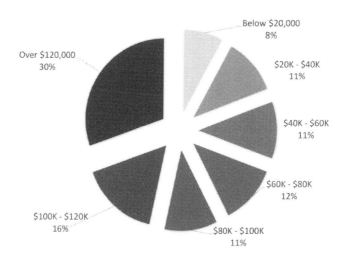

Figure 7. Medical school admissions process favors applicants from high income families.

A striking observation, 57% of accepted applicants in the United States come from families earning over $80,000/year, while 60% of U.S. households make less than $75,000/year. Even more remarkable, 30% of those accepted come from households making over $120,000/year, while only 9% of the general population in the U.S. makes over $100,000/year (we noticed similar trends in our Canadian study).

That is not all. It turns out that 54% of respondents in our study identified as Caucasian, with 39% of them coming from families earning over $120,000/year. This was the highest proportion of all groups. In fact, 69% of respondents from families earning over $100,000/year identified as Caucasians. Alternately, 61% of those identifying as visible minorities were from families earning less than $80,000/year (Figure 8).

Comparison of Family Income Distribution of Caucasian, Asian, and Visible Minority Medical School Students and Residents at the Time of Application to Medical School

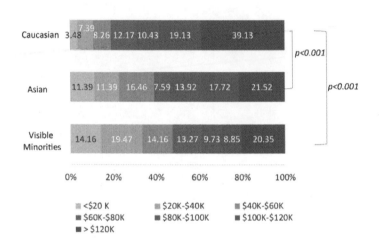

Family Income at the Time of Application (CAD)

Figure 8. Medical school admissions process favors applicants from high income families. 39.13% of Caucasian respondents came from families making >$120,000/year, the highest proportion of all groups, a significantly higher income breakdown compared to Asians, and other visible minorities.

Furthermore, applicants from higher income families appeared to receive more than one acceptance more often, as compared to lower income applicants, giving them more varied choice and the freedom to choose their future medical school (Figure 9). Notably, while the data shown in Figure 9 did not reach statistical significance in our US study, the same data was statistically significant in Canada with a P value of 0.01.

Percentage of Medical School Students and Residents Receiving More Than One Acceptance

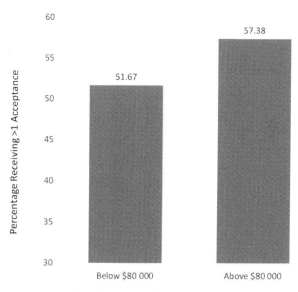

Figure 9. Medical school applicants from households with over $80,000 annual income appear to receive more than 1 acceptance more often compared to those from households with less than $80,000 annual income.

Third, and most important, it appears that the majority (68–75%) of accepted applicants are primarily motivated by wealth, status, or because one or more family members are/had been doctors or other health care professionals. Only 25–33% appear to be purely intrinsically motivated to pursue medicine without the need for external rewards or pressures (Figure 10).

Single Most Important Factor for Pursuing a Career in Medicine

Why did you apply to medical school? Please indicate the single most important factor to you.

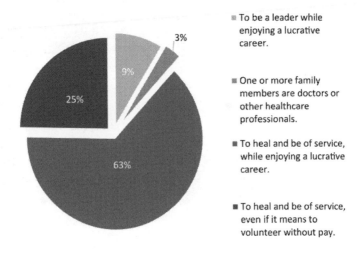

Figure 10. Majority (75%) of medical school students and residents indicate to be primarily motivated by extrinsic factors such as wealth, status, and familial pressure.

Our results are similar to an AAMC survey of graduating medical students,[78] where students were asked the following question: "How influential were the following in helping you choose your specialty?" The choices included extrinsic motives such as "income expectations." The results show that year after year, only ~22% of respondents chose income as bearing "no influence" on their decision to choosing a specialty, implying that only 22% were intrinsically motivated regardless of the monetary reward. This provides a layer of validation to our studies. This is what I believe to be the most important finding, since motivation directs behavior and is therefore the best predictor of future on-the-job performance. Notably, intrinsic motivation does not correlate with wealth or racial background (Figure 11). Thus, a primary goal of any admissions screening tool must be the ability to detect the applicants' level of *intrinsic* motivation; yet, it is clear that no current admissions tool can discern the level of intrinsic motivation in applicants, which is unsurprising as they have not been designed to do so. Instead, screening practices have focused on detecting personal and professional characteristics or cognitive abilities, which are less than ideal measures for predicting future behavior due to the context principle and socioeconomic bias; furthermore, they miss the fundamental point that behavior is directed by motivation and not by "professionalism" or standardized test scores.

Correlation of Intrinsic Motivation with Family Income & Racial Background

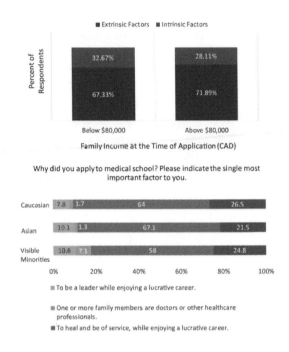

Figure 11. Intrinsic motivation does not significantly correlate with family income (top) or racial background (bottom).

Lastly, the observed trends in our studies were ubiquitous, regardless of the type of admissions screening tool used; we did not find any notable differences in reported trends based on the admissions screening tool used to select future doctors. These tools included the use of situational judgment tests such as CASPer and MMIs, the MCAT, personal statements, and reference letters (Figure 2).

Motivation of Medical School Students and Residents Selected Using Different Admissions Interviews Formats & Situational Judgment Tests

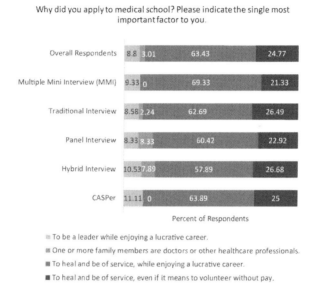

Why did you apply to medical school? Please indicate the single most important factor to you.

- To be a leader while enjoying a lucrative career.
- One or more family members are doctors or other healthcare professionals.
- To heal and be of service, while enjoying a lucrative career.
- To heal and be of service, even if it means to volunteer without pay.

Figure 2. 75% of medical school students and residents indicate that the primary reason for pursuing a career in medicine is due to extrinsic factors such as wealth, status, or familial pressure regardless of the admissions screening tool used to select them.

For further details with regards to these studies, visit the following 2 links:

US study: https://sortsmart.io/blog/united-states-medical-school-admissions-study

Canadian study: https://sortsmart.io/blog/canadian-medical-school-admissions-study

To watch my BSI conference presentation summarizing these results, visit the link below:

> https://www.youtube.com/watch?v=irDvhC7CE_k

To watch my TEDx talk, visit the link below:

> https://www.youtube.com/watch?v=BjC7cM8a5zU

These 2 studies were followed by a third, a year later, to examine whether the use of situational judgment tests such as CASPer and MMI at McMaster University had made any significant difference or improvements to the observed bias. Although the above studies demonstrated that situational judgment tests do not appear to fare any better, it was important to explore this at McMaster itself, since it could be argued that the variations of situational judgment tests and how they are used in the selection process might impact their efficacies.[75] Moreover, McMaster University appears to claim that such situational judgment tests are better than other forms of traditional screening practices and advocates for their spread to other universities. In fact, they have gone as far as creating spin-off ventures for their commercialization.

At the time of writing this book, McMaster University's medical school admissions office appears to claim that the best way to select applicants is using the following "selection formulae" on its website:

"FORMULA 1: INVITATION TO INTERVIEW:

- 32% Undergraduate Grade Point Average

- 32% MCAT Verbal Reasoning OR Critical Analysis and Reasoning Score

- 32% CASPer Score

- 4% Graduate Degree Bonus (1% Master's/4% PhD)

FORMULA 2: ADVANCEMENT TO
COLLATION/OFFER OF ADMISSION:

- 70% Multiple Mini Interview Score

- 15% Undergraduate Grade Point Average

- 15% MCAT Verbal Reasoning OR Critical Analysis
  and Reasoning Score"

Notwithstanding the lack of empirical proof for the use of such percentages in the selection criteria, our results indicate no significant difference between applicants accepted to McMaster University, as compared to other Canadian medical schools.

Similar to other medical schools in Canada, McMaster University's accepted applicants appeared to be mostly extrinsically motivated (Figure 12) and from families with significantly higher incomes than the general population (Figure 13). These results suggest that the use of situational judgment tests introduced by McMaster do not appear to perform any better, compared to other admissions screening protocols, to promote diversity.

**Primary Motivation of Medical School Applicants
Accepted to McMaster Medical School in Comparison to
Those Accepted to Other Canadian Medical Schools**

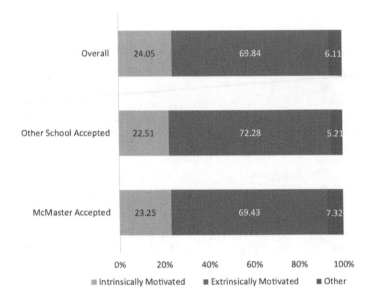

Figure 12. Similar to other Canadian medical schools, the majority (69%) of accepted applicants to McMaster medical school are partially or completely extrinsically motivated to pursue medicine by status, financial gain, or familial tradition or pressure.

Family Income Distribution of Applicants Accepted to McMaster Medical School in Comparison to Those Accepted to Other Canadian Medical Schools

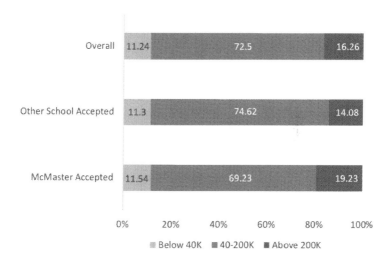

Figure 13. Similar to other Canadian medical schools, a significant proportion (19%) of accepted applicants to McMaster medical school are from families with income in excess of $200K/year with 50% from families with an annual income of $100K/year or more. In comparison, the median family household income in Canada is $70,336/year, according to Statistics Canada.

We dug deeper to study the impact of the use of GPA, MCAT CARS, CASPer, and MMI during the screening process, all part of McMaster's admissions process.

As highlighted in Figure 14 and 15, higher GPA and MCAT CARS scores correlate directly with family income.

Applicants from lower income families are significantly disadvantaged by such selection criteria.

Family Income and MCAT CARS/Verbal Reasoning Correlation in Medical School Applicants

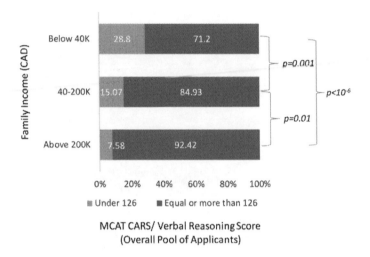

Figure 14. MCAT CARS scores directly correlate with family income in medical school applicants. Applicants from families with income in excess of $200K/year score significantly higher on the Critical Analysis and Reasoning Skills (CARS) or the Verbal Reasoning section of the Medical College Admission Test (MCAT), compared to those from families earning $40-200K/year, which in turn have higher scores compared to those from families earning below $40K/year.

Family Income and GPA Correlation in Medical School Applicants

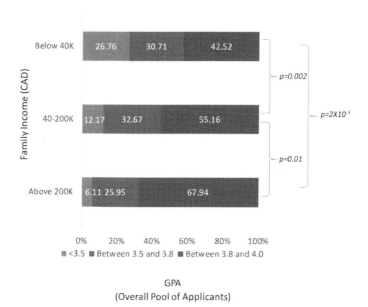

Figure 15. GPA directly correlates with family income in medical school applicants. Applicants from families earning over $200K/year have significantly higher GPA scores compared to those from families earning $40-200K/year, which in turn have higher GPA scores, compared to those from families earning below $40K/year.

While this study does not provide direct insight about the cause of the bias, one possible explanation for such bias is due to more free time afforded by applicants from higher income families to dedicate to academic performance, since they are not forced to work multiple jobs to pay their tuition or rent.

Figure 16 and 17 indicate that selection based on CASPer and MMIs also appear to correlate with wealth. The data depicts that individuals selected using CASPer or MMIs were, on average, from higher income families. The wealth distribution of those selected using these tests did not appear to differ from the wealth distribution of applicants selected without them. Given that we did not have access to the CASPer and MMI scores for each applicant, it was not possible to conclude whether CASPer and MMI are directly contributing to the observed bias. However, the observed trend minimally suggests that the use of CASPer and MMI does not significantly help ameliorate the reported wealth bias using other traditional admissions screening protocols. Furthermore, this observation is in agreement with previous studies, suggesting that individuals with higher socioeconomic status normally perform better on such admissions tests.[69,70,72]

Lastly, when we examined the correlation between MCAT CARS, GPA, CASPer and MMI with intrinsic motivation, we were not able to find any statistically significant correlations, suggesting the inability of any of these tools to detect motivation in applicants. While the study showed no statistically significant correlations, there was an interesting trend worth noting. Greater percentage of applicants with lower GPA or MCAT CARS scores appeared to be intrinsically motivated compared to those with higher scores, implying an inverse relationship between GPA and MCAT CARS scores and intrinsic motivation! My prediction is that a similar pattern would have emerged for CASPer and MMI scores if we had access to such data. The data hints that pressures of such admissions tools may cause applicants to be mostly motivated by test performance rather than the joy of the profession itself, leading to decreased intrinsic motivation, a notion supported by multiple independent research studies.[123,124]

For full study details, visit the following link: https://sortsmart.io/blog/mcmaster-study

Family Income Distribution of Medical School Students and Residents Selected With or Without the Use of Multiple Mini Interview

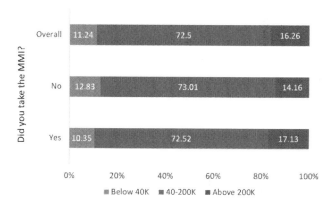

Family Income at the Time of Application (CAD)

Figure 16. Multiple mini interview (MMI) does not appear to show any significant advantage in its ability to promote wealth diversity compared to other admissions screening tools. A significant proportion (17%) of accepted applicants screened using MMI are from families with an income in excess of $200K/year.

Family Income Distribution of Medical School Students and Residents Selected With or Without the Use of CASPer

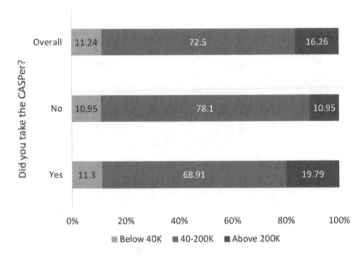

Family Income at the Time of Application (CAD)

Figure 17. CASPer does not appear to show any significant advantage in its ability to promote wealth diversity compared to other admissions screening processes. A significant proportion (20%) of accepted applicants screened using CASPer are from families with an income in excess of $200K/year.

Chapter III

So What's a "Good" Admissions Screening Test?

"Any intelligent fool can make things bigger and more complex... It takes a touch of genius—and a lot of courage—to move in the opposite direction."
—E. F. Schumacher

We spent the last 2 chapters talking about the advent of admissions screening and the problem with existing practices. Before we discuss the design of a better admissions screening procedure, we must define a good test. But what does a good admissions screening test entail? It should allow one to consistently select top-performing students with the highest likelihood of future on-the-job success, while simultaneously promoting diversity.

Therefore, a good test must be able to accomplish all the following:

1) It must predict future on-the-job behavior and performance, not just future test scores.

2) It must assess the level of intrinsic motivation, since motivation predicts future behavior.

3) It must assess conscientiousness and coachability as the only other 2 proven qualities linked to future on-the-job success.

4) It must respect each applicant's individuality to promote diversity and prevent selection of similar groups of individuals, which would lead to group-think.

5) It must avoid introducing any implicit bias in the admissions process related to race, gender, cultural, socioeconomic background, or any other variable irrelevant to future career success.

6) It must have strong validity to measure what it is supposed to—in our case, future on-the-job behavior.

7) It must have strong reliability and be able to produce consistent, reliable results in any program/institution.

8) It must allow for the screening of the entire applicant pool using the same exact procedure.

9) It must allow for the numeric scoring of each applicant's performance for quantitative analysis.

10) It must be easy to implement.

11) It must be both cost and time effective.

To achieve this, you and your admissions team would have to adopt new strategies, abandoning certain other opposing practices, if currently in use. This change is initially going to feel difficult—the transition might seem uncomfortable, but that is a good sign! It implies that you are fighting the urge to adhere to the status quo in favor of experimenting with something new. Whatever the case, I urge you to experiment with the following strategies, at least for one admission cycle. You have absolutely nothing to lose and everything to gain—your future students, institution administrators, stakeholders, and, most importantly, the public will thank you for the bold initiative and for sustaining the vision to introduce positive change when the opportunity presents itself.

A Swiss Army knife with just 3 blades: How to remove complexity and focus on The Big Three

Since the introduction of the first standardized test by Thorndike in early 1900s, much progress has been made in admissions screening. More standardized tests, personal statements, short essays, letters of recommendations, situational judgment tests, traditional interviews, mini interviews, and hybrid interviews have been implemented, to name a few. Interestingly, some universities now use a combination of most of these practices. It is as if the admissions process has become more complex and bloated. We tend to add anything we hear about, rather than pausing and re-evaluating old habits. The reality is that it is always best to *remove* complexity to make a process more efficient and better, rather than adding more steps. Yet, it is much harder to remove steps than add them. For example, imagine if Apple kept continuously adding to its technology. Let's consider the iPhone. Let's say Apple added more batteries, more cameras, a printer, a fax machine, a keyboard, a mouse, an old school wired headset, a visible and bulky antenna, and so on. It seems absurd, doesn't it? Instead, Apple has been carefully removing more and more. It has removed the buttons; it has removed the need to buy a separate music player; it has removed the antenna; it has even removed wires from its headphones. I believe the same strategy can be applied to any admissions screening process.

There are 2 fundamental ways to reduce complexity from your admissions process:

1) Streamlining your actual process into 1 single step, and

2) Focusing on a few select qualities to look for in your applicants, instead of 10 or 20.

The streamlining of the admissions process is a lot easier than people think; I will discuss this in the next section. This will be one of the most important sections of this chapter.

Focusing on a handful of qualities or less, on the other hand, is more challenging. Traditionally, most admissions practices have had a long list of qualities to screen for in prospective students. This is not surprising given the inherent risk of errors and the inability to select a few characteristics most likely to predict future behavior. For example, the American Association of Medical Colleges (AAMC) lists 15 "core competencies" and the Federation of Law Societies of Canada lists 11 qualities for a "competent lawyer," one of which has 8 sub-categories.

But what if I told you that you only need to screen your applicants for 3 qualities? Not 20, 15, or even 5—just 3.

I call these "The Big Three" (as opposed to The Big Five popularized in psychology); they include intrinsic motivation, conscientiousness, and coachability. There is overwhelming evidence in the literature indicating that individuals who possess these qualities can and will acquire any other auxiliary skill and personality trait to help them in the pursuit of their profession. I will provide additional details about each of these traits in the upcoming sections.

The remainder of this chapter is broken down into distinct sections denoted as specific "Rules." Each rule is fundamental to design a scientifically sound and fair admissions process.

Rule 1

Less is More: Screen Your Entire Pool of Applicants by Streamlining Your Admissions Process into a Single Step and Eliminating "Rolling Admissions"

"Perfection is not when there is no more to add, but no more to take away."

—Antoine de Saint-Exupéry

The first step is to create a system or tool that allows you to screen your entire pool of applicants. This is critical to create a scientific and fair admissions process. Consequently, this is also the best way to find needles in haystacks, while eliminating the need for rolling admissions.

Let us assume you were literally sorting through a stack of hay, looking for needles. What are your options?

A. You create a sorting device or mechanism that allows you to sift through the *entire* stack, or

B. You sort through manually; in which case you'll be forced to first arbitrarily narrow down the portion of hay you need to sort through to save time. For example, you will narrow down the amount by the shade of needles, their length, their location, or other random criteria.

Which of these 2 methods are *guaranteed* to help you find the needles? As you probably must have agreed, only option A is going to guarantee you find every single needle. Option B might find you some of the needles but may also result in no needles being found.

I will provide you with another example of this in nature. I will use biology, and specifically immunology because of my educational background. I believe nature has figured out all the fundamental laws already; all we need to do to be successful is find the connections and use them in our everyday lives.

Your immune system is composed of specialized cells, such as T cells, that are continuously circulating your bloodstream and looking for foreign invaders. Each T cell has a unique T cell receptor with a unique affinity to foreign particles or antigens. This is done intentionally, to maximize the chances of finding any possible combination of foreign microorganisms. When a T cell finds a correct antigen, it binds to it and starts proliferating to mount an immune response that ultimately eliminates the invading microorganisms associated with that specific antigen. Note, our immune system does not arbitrarily choose a specific part of the blood to screen—it certainly does not randomly choose where to screen. Instead, it actively and continuously monitors our entire body for signs of invasions; as a result, it can detect and eliminate harmful entities from our body, most of the time, before it is too late.

The admissions process is much the same, albeit more elegant and more sensitive, since we are dealing with real people, with real hopes and real futures. The only way to determine who is best suited for your program is to assess the suitability of *all* applicants across multiple independent variables before making a decision. For example, if you are using traditional applicant screening, such as standardized tests and in-person interviews, you must administer both the standardized test and the interview to your *entire* pool of applicants before making a final decision, since you might miss out on great candidates who do extremely well on interviews but may not do well on standardized testing, or vice versa. Your job is to ensure every applicant's performance is scored on your standardized test and interview. Importantly, the 2 tests must be independent of each other—they must be rated using different evaluators who do not know the applicants' scores on any previous tests. For example, interviewers must not know the applicants' standardized test scores, while the standardized test raters should not know the applicants' interview scores. This process will eliminate inadvertent bias. In this scenario, you'll have 2 independent scores for each applicant, which can be used to make a more holistic admissions decision that is fairer and more scientific. Of course, both the standardized testing and the traditional interviews are strategies you should phase out of your screening process, for reasons discussed earlier; however, they do provide a great way for me to illustrate my point here.

But you might be thinking, "How are we to conduct in-person interviews for thousands and maybe tens of thousands during each admissions cycle? This would require unreasonable resources in the form of time and money."

I completely understand the predicament. The process is already time-consuming to prohibit change. I would like to share an example to illustrate this point.

While finalizing the manuscript for this book, I interviewed the Director of Admissions at the Case Western Reserve University, School of Dental Medicine, Dr. Emil Chuck. Dr. Chuck draws upon his own training as a scientist and is always looking for new ways to promote diversity. This is probably why he was one of the first people to contact me directly inquiring about SortSmart. In our interview, he revealed that, on average their admissions team spends roughly 1,250 hours screening approximately 2,500 applicants during *each* application cycle. Assuming an 8-hour workday, 5 days a week, that is equivalent to more than half a *year* spent screening applicants during each application cycle! Notably, this is the amount of time that goes into the pre-interview stage alone. Imagine spending more than half a year screening applicants while giving most applicants only 10 minutes or less, especially those that have not been selected for in-person interviews.

Sadly, this is a typical scenario. If you do the math, you will notice that a lot of your time is being spent on applicant screening while using traditional methods; I estimate that if you were to implement the strategies in this book, it would require you at least 100 to 1,000 times more time, money, and energy. As a result, you will likely give up and go back to old habits that are hurting your admissions process and your efforts to promote diversity.

That is exactly what almost happened to us. When we first learned these strategies, we realized we were spending more and more time on applicant screening. Frankly, we got really tired after a few months because while the strategies were working perfectly, all of our time and money was going into selecting new team members. The process was inefficient and not scalable. This is what led us to create the SortSmart software to automate the entire process.

Instead of relying on ineffective in-person interviews or other traditional applicant screening practices, you have to create an admissions process to be completed in a single step, using an online software to speed up the process; this allows all applicants to participate remotely, regardless of their geographical location. Of course, this would require years of research and development if you were to develop it on your own. However, this type of technology is now readily available and highly reliable. For example, the free software we created at SortSmart allows screening of all applicants simultaneously in an afternoon. Imagine screening your entire pool of applicants in just 60 minutes!

Streamlining the process will greatly enhance the efficiency and fairness of your admissions screening, but in order to best predict future behavior, you must focus on assessing applicants based on intrinsic motivation, coachability, and conscientiousness, each of which will be discussed in Rules 2, 3, and 4, respectively.

Rule 2

Select Intrinsically Motivated Applicants Who Are Willing to Pursue the Profession with Blood, Sweat, and Tears, Even If It Means to Simply Volunteer

"Pleasure in the job puts perfection in the work."
—Aristotle

Imagine you could select students genuinely interested in pursuing the profession and in serving others, rather than those primarily motivated by financial gain, status, or social pressure. Wouldn't that be sufficient, rather than having a list of 15 different "core competencies"?

Let us take a step back. The objective of your admissions process is to select students more likely to behave in certain ways, both during training and later as future professionals. Therefore, the best way is to screen applicants based on a quality that directs behavior. What directs our behavior? What causes people to act? What causes people to develop all the personality traits that are required to perform the job well?

Motivation directs behavior or *moves* people to action. It is the precursor to any behavior. We are likely to engage in an activity and display certain behaviors when motivated by social pressure, rewards, fear, or status; moreover, perhaps we are motivated because we find the activity itself rewarding.

The Self-Determination Theory (SDT) of motivation, pioneered by Edward Deci and Richard Ryan and dating back to 1975, divides motivation into 2 main classifications—intrinsic and extrinsic.[79,80] Intrinsic motivation is defined as the desire to engage in an activity that is rewarding on its own, regardless of external rewards, such as monetary rewards, status, or social pressure. Psychologist Mihaly Csikszentmihalyi, in his best-selling book *Flow: The Psychology of Optimal Experience*, describes this theory of optimal experience as "the state in which people are so involved in an activity that nothing else seems to matter; the experience itself is so enjoyable that people will do it even at great cost, for the sheer sake of doing it."[81]

For example, if you think back to your childhood, the copious amounts of time you spent playing video games or playing with your toys are examples of intrinsic motivation. You probably did not require any external pressure to engage in such activities. In fact, if you were like me—you probably persisted despite external pressures, such as your parents' advice to stop so you could finish your homework instead. This is exactly how I became a master at playing

Super Mario; but eventually, I had to drop first year physics—apparently those video game moves have absolutely nothing to do with real world physics!

On the other hand, extrinsic motivation is defined as the desire to engage in an activity due to external pressures such as rewards, status, social pressure, and fear.[79,80] The behavior is normally discontinued as soon as the external pressures are removed or replaced by a different behavior, given new and greater external and/or internal pressures. For example, someone primarily motivated by financial gain will readily quit their current job for a new one with a larger salary.

Intrinsically-motivated behaviors are autonomous; extrinsically-motivated behaviors are controlled or coerced by either internal or external factors. However, some forms of extrinsic motivation can be internalized and in return become autonomous through one's acceptance of external values. In such circumstances, the behavior becomes autonomous not because it is a joy on its own, but to avoid self-shame, disappointment, or a damaged ego.

Importantly, people with genuine or self-authored motivation, when compared to those externally controlled to act, have more interest, excitement, and confidence, and end up experiencing enhanced performance, persistence, creativity, self-esteem, and general well-being. This process creates an autonomous, positive feedback loop with continuous engagement in the same activity; it may lead to mastery in any field. This is true, even when people have the same competence or efficacy for the activity. Thus, it is critical to be able to discern the level of intrinsic vs. extrinsic motivation of applicants during the admissions process.

Conversely, when people are primarily motivated by extrinsic factors such as wealth, fame, and image, they tend to be less psychologically healthy, learn inadequately, and perform poorly.

Generally, a sense of competence, autonomy, self-improvement, relatedness, and challenge lead to increased levels of intrinsic motivation, whereas control, lack of competence actualization, and external rewards decrease it. These concepts are best understood through a brief review of work in this field. In the following paragraphs, I will provide examples from studies across relevant disciplines including sports, health care, work, and, importantly, education. I highly recommend you review these case studies, especially those related to work and education—they have a direct impact on applicant screening and selection in university admissions. I will end this section with specific strategies to detect the level of intrinsic motivation in applicants.

Sports

Sports is the perfect subject to study motivation. From birth, humans seek physical activity. It is not only self-rewarding, but essential for both biological and cognitive development, and thus intrinsically motivating. While regular, planned exercise is not intrinsically motivating, people almost exclusively engage in sports due to their intrinsic motivation to play, optimally challenge themselves, and compete against peers.[82-85] For most, participating in sports is joyous and even used as a stress reliever. Continuous participation often leads to improved performance, which in turn encourages further participation in the same activities. Normally, participation is voluntary—it enhances the level of intrinsic motivation and leads to more of the same activity. Thus, we may see people with well-paying jobs engage in sports or leisurely physical activity without any external reward and, at times, at the expense of their job performance. Similarly, we see students who do poorly in school, but excel in sports.

Generally, engagement in sports is supported by intrinsic motivation, whereas participation in exercise is driven by extrinsic motivation.[82-85] For example, a study by Raedeke et al. showed that adolescent swimmers driven by intrinsic motivation experienced less burnout, as compared to those extrinsically motivated to participate in the activity.[86] Many studies have repeated these results, several indicating that when people engage in sports for external rewards, pressures from coaches and parents, or scholarships, their level of intrinsic motivation is diminished, to the point where they may no longer participate when external pressures are removed. For example, Orlick and Mosher showed that when children were offered a reward for a previously intrinsically-motivating motor balancing task, the children spent less time engaging in the activity without the reward compared to baseline and those who were not rewarded.[87] It thus comes as no wonder that sports have created many intrinsically motivated athletes who seem to defy what is biologically possible—Michael Jordan, Wayne Gretzky, Michael Phelps, Serena Williams, Tiger Woods, Usain Bolt, and Katie Ledecky are few of the most famous.

Health care

Achieving health is an innate and seemingly intrinsic desire. Yet, in complex health issues, people are not intrinsically motivated to follow the advice of their health care providers or consistent in taking prescribed medications. Research has demonstrated that adherence to recommended therapeutic intervention is greatly enhanced when practitioners are autonomy-supportive, educating their patients in an understanding manner rather than forcing their expertise. This has been shown consistently in different fields, such as weight loss, diabetes, smoking cessation, dental care, and medication adherence.[88–98]

Notably, Williams and Deci found that when medical students were trained using an autonomy-supportive teaching style, they were more likely to provide autonomy-supportive care to their patients.[99] Furthermore, the practitioners showed an increased level of intrinsic motivation to learn, which continued beyond their formal training, performed better, and experienced less burnout or turnover intentions, as we will soon see in the subsequent sections on work and education.

It is unsurprising that autonomy is a central ethical concept in many professions, which requires professionals to respect individual autonomy, allowing their patients or clients to think, decide, and act autonomously after being educated via informed consent. Therefore, it is imperative to select applicants who are intrinsically motivated; furthermore, it is important to enhance this motivation during training and teach them to support the autonomy of those under their care.

Work

Work constitutes a substantial part of our lives. On average, people spend 10 hours each day at work and in commuting. It is also an essential aspect of life. Aside from a source of income required for survival, people are driven by a sense of fulfillment; work often gives people a sense of purpose. Some are completely immersed in their work—the lines between life and work become blurry for them. Yet, most people think of work as something they *must* do to pay the bills and normally cannot wait until the week is over. In fact, studies have shown that worker productivity is low across industries on Fridays, whereas Mondays experience the greatest number of sick days.[100–101] Given the explicit nature of an extrinsic motivator in the form of monetary reward tightly associated with work, how is work influenced by intrinsic motivation? The sense of autonomy, competence, and connectedness to a community is crucial for promoting intrinsic motivation, which leads to increased proactivity, productivity, commitment, and better job performance as many studies have found.

These ideas are supported by the research of several independent scientists in the field. For example, Fernet et al. discovered that self-motivated employees showed greater job commitment and felt less emotional exhaustion.[102] Otis and Pelletier found that police officers who perceived their supervisors as autonomy-supportive were more self-motivated, experienced less physical symptoms, and were less likely to show signs of turnover intention.[103] In 2 independent studies of teachers in Gambia and China, researchers found that when teachers were autonomously motivated, they performed better and experienced both greater job satisfaction and life satisfaction.[104–105] In a study of tenured professors, Becker, et al. found that intrinsically-motivated professors were more committed to their research, spending more hours on their work.[106]

On the other hand, lack of managerial support and the sense of autonomy leads to poor on-the-job performance. Fernet et al. showed in 2 independent studies, that school teachers and nurses lacking autonomy owed to aggressive supervisor monitoring experienced more emotional exhaustion, burnout, and increased turnover intentions.[107–108]

Similarly, a focus on extrinsic motivators, such as pay, tends to negatively impact both psychological health and performance. Vansteenkiste et al. showed in a study of 900 Belgian workers that when workers were mostly motivated by pay, job security, and vacation time vs. those that found their job interesting and optimally challenging, they were less satisfied with their jobs, less happy in life, experienced added emotional exhaustion, and showed increased turnover intentions. Interestingly, while individuals with higher salaries were happier than those with lower salaries, high earning, extrinsically-motivated employees were less satisfied and happy than those who were intrinsically motivated.[109] Van den Broeck et al. found that extrinsically-motivated employees showed less flexibility in the workplace, which is essential for long term success of any organization due to continuously changing challenges.[110]

Fernet et al. showed that university professors enjoying a greater decisional control experienced positive differences only when they too showed higher levels of autonomous motivation.[111] This is an important fact to note and we're going to return to it later, since it shows that while autonomy enhances intrinsic motivation, it does not *cause* it. Thus, it is important to select individuals who are intrinsically motivated during the admissions process, rather than trying to motivate those who are extrinsically motivated.

Education

Early on in life, education and learning are intrinsically-motivated behaviors. Children learn through imitation, curiosity, and play; they find the process of exploring and discovering new information about themselves and their surrounding naturally enjoyable, since this promotes self-improvement. In formal schooling and education, however, the style of teaching, parenting, and curriculum have a significant impact on the intrinsic vs. extrinsic motivators of learning. Intrinsic motivation is enhanced when students experience autonomy over their learning, while extrinsic motivation is largely involved when students are mostly driven by grades, social comparison, rewards, and punishments. Ultimately, the goal of schooling is not only to help students autonomously gravitate toward subject matters of self-interest, but to learn the relevant cognitive and non-cognitive skills required for their future, adult lives. Such a goal can only be accomplished in an environment that supports intrinsic motivation and limits the use of extrinsic motivators, as research across ages and cultures have consistently demonstrated.

Danner and Lonky showed in a study that intrinsic motivation is correlated with active learning and cognitive growth.[112] Another study showed college students who were intrinsically motivated performed better on an unexpected test; they found the material more interesting than students who were not intrinsically motivated.[113] A study in Canada and Sweden, showed that intrinsic motivation was positively correlated with academic achievement.[114] It was followed by another study, demonstrating that such correlation does not depend on either racial or ethnic backgrounds.[115]

Intrinsic motivation across all levels of education from high school to post-graduate training in law schools and medical schools have been shown to be supported by autonomy-supportive teaching style. Not only does this style of teaching lead to increased academic performance and psychological well-being, it is associated with reduced stress. Vansteenkiste et al. showed that autonomy-supportive teaching in high school leads to better time-management, deep learning, and persistence.[116] Black and Deci showed that autonomy-supportive teaching in an undergraduate organic chemistry course led to higher competence, reduced stress, and higher scores in the course.[117] In medical school, autonomy support has been shown to enhance learning, leading to better on-the-job performance.[118]   Moreover,   autonomy   support   by preceptors has been shown to positively influence medical students' choice for residency training. For example, in a study of students from 3 American medical schools, students who found their surgery preceptor more autonomy-supportive than their internal medicine preceptor, were more likely to select surgery for their residency training.[119] In law school, the autonomy-supportive instruction style has been found to lead to higher grades, better bar exam performance, and higher motivation in the first job after graduation.[120]

While an autonomy-supportive teaching environment enhances intrinsic motivation and learning, controlling the teaching climate reduces intrinsic motivation and hurts learning. For example, the commonplace practice of grading and standardized high stakes testing have been shown to reduce the sense of autonomy and promote extrinsically-motivated behavior and poor learning.

Grolnick and Ryan showed in a study of elementary school students that when students were told they were going to be graded on an assigned reading, they performed worse on deep, conceptual learning; they forgot more of the memorized facts 1 week after the test, as compared to students who were not told they were going to be tested or graded.[121] In another study by Benware and Deci, college students who were told they would be tested on a neurophysiology text performed worse on the conceptual questions and found the material less interesting as compared to another group of peers who were informed they would not be tested but were given an opportunity to teach the material to their peers.[122] Grades generally lead students to narrowly focus on the material being tested, instead of understanding the deeper concepts and real-world contexts.

A report by Hout and Elliot concluded that high-stakes testing does not provide an appropriate assessment of students' learning and has no impact on achievement.[123] Instead, it is associated with the pressures of rewards and punishments, extrinsic motivators of behavior, thus leading to less enjoyment, decreased autonomy, and poor performance.[124] *

As we have seen, intrinsically-motivated individuals are more committed to their work, experience job and life satisfaction, do not suffer burnout, bear fewer turnover tendencies, are more flexible, and, most importantly, perform better. We have also learned that the best way to foster intrinsic motivation is by creating an autonomy-supportive environment that promotes a sense of relatedness and provides an ongoing optimal challenge. Lastly, we have seen that it is not possible to ignite intrinsic motivation in individuals, rather it is only possible to enhance the same in individuals who already have an intrinsic drive for the profession. Therefore, it is now clear why it is critical to select applicants intrinsically motivated to pursue a profession. But how can one detect the level of intrinsic versus extrinsic motivation in applicants?

How to detect intrinsic motivation

The best way to design procedures and questions to detect intrinsic motivation is to think back about the definition of intrinsic versus extrinsic motivation. Here are the definitions again:

> Intrinsic motivation is the desire to engage in an activity that is self-rewarding on its own regardless of

---

* For further reading about intrinsic motivation and SDT, refer to the 2 books written by Richard M. Ryan and Edward L. Deci,[79,80] which provide a comprehensive overview of plethora of research spanning over 40 years and applications in multiple domains.

external rewards, whereas extrinsic motivation is when the desire to engage in an activity is driven by the aspiration to attain some sort of reward, such as money, fame, status, or recognition, or by avoiding punishment. Motivation, whether extrinsic or intrinsic is what influences action and behavior. Therefore, if you have a better understanding of the motivation of your applicants, you will have a better chance of predicting future behavior.

Most complex behaviors, such as the decision to apply to a professional program, are the result of both intrinsic and extrinsic motivations. Thus, the focus of any applicant screening procedure should be to detect *both* intrinsic and extrinsic motivation. Once you know the level of each, you can decide which applicants are more likely to perform better during their training and in their future jobs.

There are 2 ways to detect the levels of intrinsic versus extrinsic motivation. The first is using questions specifically designed to detect motivation. The other is by inferences from all other types of questions that may not be specifically designed to detect motivation. The latter is actually the best way to detect genuine motivation; however, it is also the hardest and requires trained eyes and ears in addition to a database of tens of thousands of answers from many different individuals whose level of motivation is pre-determined. My goal would be to teach you how to detect motivation using both methods based on my experience at SortSmart.

The general framework for designing questions and assessing responses is discussed in Rule #13 and chapters IV and V. I have created these chapters as a quick guide you can return to over and over again. I have intentionally arranged those chapters to appear towards the end of the book, because I would like to illustrate how this is done in the context of different questions before providing the raw formula; you will appreciate that elements of the framework are repeated throughout this book and can be applied to any question type.

Designing questions that directly detect motivation: The stealth fun formula

The goal here is to ask questions that detect the *genuine* level of motivation for each applicant. This is challenging because if the applicant knows you are trying to detect motivation, they will do their best to make themselves appear motivated, the same problem faced using traditional applicant screening questions. There are 2 ways to accomplish this. The first, is to ensure that your questions do not reveal that they are meant to detect intrinsic motivation. The second, ensure the applicant is providing their response under specific time pressures. I will discuss the former below and we will revisit the latter in Rule #6 because it deserves an entire section and applies to all possible questions and procedures.

The stealth fun formula

The stealth fun formula is meant to ask questions that allow you to detect what the applicant likes to do for fun in a subtle manner. All you have to do is create questions that assess what the applicant finds enjoyable, because intrinsically motivating activities are first and foremost enjoyable. But the idea is not to uncover everything your applicants do for fun; instead, you want to focus on the aspects of the profession that they find exciting. Furthermore, you want to do this in a way that doesn't broadcast your intention to detect their level of intrinsic motivation. Lastly, any questions you create must allow you to discern poor responses from good ones using a numeric scale, a topic further developed in Rule #7.

Let us review a few examples of poor questions versus excellent questions to break down the process.

Poor questions:

- "What is your level of intrinsic motivation to pursue medicine?"

- "What is more important to you: job security or serving others?"

- "Why do you want to become a dentist?"

What is your level of intrinsic motivation to pursue medicine?

This is a terrible question—it is clearly not stealthy; it is not possible to discern good versus poor answers and it is certainly not possible to assign a numeric score to any such response.

What is more important to you: job security or serving others?

Almost 100% of applicants will recognize that the socially acceptable response is "serving others." Therefore, this question is dead before it has a chance. It also fails by not allowing the use of a numeric scoring system to differentiate applicants. It is mostly a black and white answer. Your applicants are forced to choose from 2 closed options. There is no room for debate and, as a result, there is no room for assigning a numeric scale to score your applicants' response. In general, it is never a good idea to ask a closed question that does not allow a broad variation in responses.

Why do you want to become a dentist?

This is a common question used in any profession: "Why do you want to become x, y, or z?" You can bet that most applicants have the answer to this question already memorized—rehearsed and polished. Unlike the other 2 questions, this question does have the potential to become an excellent question with some clever modifications, as you will see next.

Excellent questions:

- "What are your 5 most important reasons to pursue a law degree?"

- "If you are not accepted this year, what are your backup plans?"

- "On a scale of 1-7, 1 being least influential and 7 being most influential, please rate each of the following in their influence on your decision to pursue a career in medicine.

  - I find serving others enjoyable and fun.

  - I enjoy the income security.

  - The profession allows me to reach my family expectations.

  - I want to be a respected member of society.

  - I find scientific discovery challenging and enjoyable.

  - I enjoy having a leadership role."

What are your 5 most important reasons to pursue a law degree?

This is an excellent question—it is asking the same common question we saw earlier in a totally different way.

Instead of asking applicants why they want to pursue x or y career, it is asking them to provide their 5 most important reasons. This is going to force the applicant to provide you with 5 reasons instead of a generic, rehearsed response. Based on the applicants' response and your understanding of extrinsic vs. intrinsic motivation, you can then easily determine the level of intrinsic motivation for each applicant.

Another reason this is a great question is the vast array of responses you will receive instead of the same boring, canned responses. Using what the applicants say combined with how they say it and the order they list their 5 most important factors can be used to assign a range of numeric scores to easily differentiate among applicants.

Note: The strategies on how to score the sample questions provided throughout this book, the rationale behind their design, and sample answers from suitable vs. unsuitable applicants are provided in Chapters IV and V.

If you are not accepted this year, what are your backup plans?

This is similar to the common question, "What will you do if you are not accepted this year?" However, it has a twist. Instead of asking, "What will you do?" I'm asking another question—"What are your backup plans?" I'm intentionally assuming that the applicant has a "backup plan." This is an example of a desirable leading question that works in your favor. Again, the response reveals a lot about the applicants' true motivations and allows one to discern each applicant's true motivation using a scoring scale.

On a scale of 1–7, 1 being least influential and 7 being most influential, please rate each of the following in their influence on your decision to pursue a career in medicine.

- *I find serving others enjoyable and fun.*

- *I enjoy the income security.*

- *The profession allows me to reach my family expectations.*

- *I want to be a respected member of society.*

- *I find scientific discovery challenging and enjoyable.*

- *I enjoy having a leadership role.*

- *Other—please specify.*

These are by far my all-time favorite questions for multiple reasons. First, you notice that this is another variation to the common question, "Why do you want to pursue career x or y?" I wanted to show you that it is possible to ask this question in several different ways, to avoid canned responses. Second, I have provided a mix of intrinsic and extrinsic factors and asked the applicants to rate each option on what they consider most vs. least influential in their decision. Third, I have included an "Other" section to keep the question open-ended. This will give you yet another level of insight into the applicant's true motivation.

Now, we will turn our attention to questions that indirectly assess motivation.

Designing questions that indirectly detect motivation: The personal history formula

In general, when designing questions to test any quality, you should ask specific questions that require the applicants to respond using actual past experiences, instead of using hypothetical questions. There are multiple advantages to this. First, unlike hypothetical questions found in situational judgment tests, mini interviews, or other traditional admissions screening practices, these types of questions are not influenced by socioeconomic status. Second, this forces applicants to deliver specific examples of past experiences on the spot, so they will be less likely to have time to form fictitious stories, which allows you to learn a lot more about the way your applicants think and behave in actual situations they have encountered in the past. Third, top applicants *know* they are the better choice and they love to talk about themselves using specific past experiences. On the other hand, unsuitable applicants are generally nervous and constantly looking for ways to please you by searching for socially acceptable responses. This causes unsuitable applicants to provide a generic response to such questions instead of specific examples. Of course, keep in mind that I am generalizing here. It is possible to have suitable applicants who may experience anxiety during specific questions. Therefore, it is essential to reserve judgment about applicants' suitability until all applicants have been assessed using a range of questions.

Incidentally, the personal history formula is also favorable when designing questions to indirectly detect intrinsic motivation. Furthermore, as almost all your questions are going to be designed in this manner, you will have many opportunities to detect motivation without the knowledge of your applicants.

Excellent questions:

- "When was the last time you engaged in an activity on your own that was not part of your work or school requirement; or performed to gain experience for your application to any academic program or employment opportunity? What did you do?"

- "When was the last time you took some time off from school work? How did you spend your time during your time off?"

- "What are your thoughts about the recent report of government funding cuts for public school teachers?"

When was the last time you engaged in an activity on your own that was not part of your work or school requirement; or performed to gain experience for your application to any academic program or employment opportunity? What did you do?

Considering the definition of intrinsic vs. extrinsic motivation, it is easy to realize why this question is powerful. The question also asks about the "last time" the applicant engaged in a self-directed activity—it is not possible to get away with a generic response. For this question, the applicant is forced to reveal the timing and the type of activity they engaged in that was completely free of any external pressures.

When was the last time you took some time off from school work? How did you spend your time during your time off?

This is a variation of the previous question, except that I am asking the applicant to talk about "time off from school work." I am also asking the applicant to explain what they did during their time off and unlike the previous question, what they did might not have been fun. This allows you to detect motivation in a different light. Again, what the applicants disclose in response to this question reveals more than you might think at first glance. Since you have been reading this far, it should be easy to start seeing how responses to this question can help your admissions process.

What are your thoughts about the recent report of government funding cuts for public school teachers?

This question assesses the applicants' knowledge of current events about their future profession; it is easy to modify such a question for any program. Why is this important? It is important because intrinsically-motivated individuals tend to learn everything about their future careers. They follow every single piece of news and interesting statistic. They ask questions. They research. They obsess. Applicants who are extrinsically motivated are less likely to answer most of such questions and, if they do, their responses would lack a deep level of understanding. On the other hand, if they do panic and start researching everything, 2 things are bound to happen: a) they will find the profession boring and they might not even apply, or b) they will be fully informed about the profession before applying. I argue that both scenarios are favorable for your admissions process.

Why not stop at selection based on intrinsic motivation?

If you master selecting applicants based on intrinsic motivation, given the research, you may not need to assess any other qualities. As mentioned earlier, applicants who are intrinsically motivated will spare no effort to learn everything necessary and be successful. This will also help promote diversity, since intrinsic motivation does not correlate with wealth, race, cultural background, or gender. Moreover, it is incredibly hard to fake.

So, if selecting intrinsically motivated individuals is sufficient on its own, why am I advocating the inclusion of screening for the other 2 traits in The Big Three—namely, conscientiousness and coachability—in the following 2 sections? This is for the following 2 reasons:

1) Our goal is to assess students on multiple characteristics independently. This adds a layer of validity to your admissions process; if your raters make mistakes on a variable, there remains a chance to save the admissions process, if the other 2 characteristics are assessed correctly. Generally, the number 1 is a deadly one. Having a singular characteristic to assess, a singular form of traditional admissions test, one evaluator, one decision-maker, or one question could be lethal if any of these fail to perform as expected in the absence of any existing back-up system.

2) Although intrinsically-motivated individuals can be easily taught to be conscientious and coachable, your program might not be able to provide sufficient time for these qualities to develop. Therefore, selecting individuals with all 3 characteristics significantly increases your chances of finding the needles in haystacks.

In consideration of the foregoing, let us turn our attention to coachability.

Rule 3

Select Coachable Applicants

"If I have seen further, it is by standing upon the shoulders of giants."

—Sir Isaac Newton

The fastest and most efficient route to master any skill is learning from people who have mastered it rather than through personal trial and error. While books can act as a great source of information, they are not as efficient as a coach who can provide personalized feedback to correct course as required.

A brief look at the history of past top performers clearly demonstrates this as true in virtually any field. For example, Albert Einstein was mentored by Max Talmey, whom he met every Thursday. Marie Curie was mentored by Henri Becquerel. Mark Zuckerberg was mentored by Steve Jobs. Alexander the Great by Aristotle. Aristotle himself was mentored by Plato, who was in turn mentored by Socrates.

The point is this: Everybody needs a coach, because it is utterly nonsensical to try to recreate the wheel. But having a coach is only half the equation. The other critical half is *being coachable*.

Coachability is the ability to take expert feedback and act on it to improve and master a skill. Coachable individuals seek criticism from experienced experts in their field with humility to improve their performance. They are willing to make mistakes and be told that they were wrong without getting defensive or argumentative. Uncoachable individuals are single-minded, firmly attached to their opinions and actions. They are unwilling to listen to those with more experience and expertise. They tend to get upset and angry at feedback because they view it as a personal attack on their egos.

In support of the importance of coachability, Smither et al. in a meta-analysis study pointed out that "specifically, improvement is most likely to occur when feedback indicates that change is necessary, recipients have a positive feedback orientation, perceive a need to change their behavior, react positively to the feedback, believe change is feasible, set appropriate goals to regulate their behavior, and take actions that lead to skill and performance improvement."[125]

Notably, coachability can be thought about in its relationship with intrinsic motivation. We have seen how intrinsic motivation creates a positive feedback loop where improved performance reinforces voluntary engagement in the activity. In this context, coachability is the willingness to continuously improve one's performance. Besides obvious benefits, coachability's importance is supported by research in sports, the workplace, and education.

In a study by Guenthner et al., collegiate athletes found to be more coachable scored higher on 5 wellness dimensions of emotional, social, spiritual, intellectual, and physical well-being. Furthermore, such athletes had better concentration, goal setting, and peaking under pressure.[126]

Shannahan et al. adapted a measure of athletic coachability to salespeople in the workplace to study the relationship between coachability and sales performance. In the study, which included a representative sample of business-to-business salespeople in the United States, they show that coachability is the strongest predictor of sales performance, as compared to competitiveness and leadership styles.[127]

George et al., in a study involving family medicine residents, showed that the introduction of a learning coach significantly enhanced self-directed learning and the goal-setting skills of the residents in training.[128] In another study, Palter et al. showed that structured peer coaching can enhance laparoscopic suturing skills learning in faculty surgeons.[129]

In a meta-analysis of 18 studies, Theeboom et al. analyzed the effect of coaching intervention on performance (for example, the number of sales and supervisor job performance evaluation), well-being (for example, depression, anxiety, and burnout), coping (for example, mindfulness and self-efficacy), work attitudes (for example, job satisfaction), and self-regulations (for example, goal setting and goal attainment) within an organizational context. The results show that coaching has significant positive effects on all 5 outcomes based on the results from all independent studies examined with the authors conclusion that such results are at least partly mediated by coachability of study participants, such as their agreeableness and openness to new experiences.[130]

How should one assess coachability during the admissions process?

Measuring the level of coachability in your applicants is much easier than assessing intrinsic motivation; nevertheless, it requires a great deal of preparation and training in advance. Coachability can be assessed using direct questions during your admissions process, with the help of referees (Rule #10) and with the use of functional tests (Rule #5).

One of my favorite questions to assess coachability is adopted from Mark Murphy's book *Hiring for Attitude* (sample question #1 below). As the name implies, this book is not related to admissions screening but to hiring top performers in the workplace, which is really the ultimate goal of any admissions screening practice. Admissions process' goal is to select individuals who are going to be outstanding during their future jobs, not just during their training days. *Hiring for Attitude* provides great insight into choosing referees and designing questions, both of which I have tweaked further to tailor the considerations for admissions screening based on my personal research and experimentation.

Sample coachability question to ask your applicants #1

Here's the question. Note, this question is intentionally designed with multiple sections which should be asked in the exact sequence shown below:

> *"Who is your current or former academic or workplace boss or direct supervisor? Would you please spell their full name for us?"*

What was it like working with this individual? What do you wish they had done differently? What was something you wish you had done differently?

When we talk to this individual, what would they say are your strengths? As you probably agree, we all have many areas of improvement, what would they say are some areas of improvement for you?"

Sample coachability question to ask your applicants #2

"Could you tell us about a specific time when your supervisor, professor, or instructor provided you with feedback about your performance, but you thought it was better to take a different approach?"

Sample coachability question to ask your applicants' referees #1

"Could you tell us about a specific time when you provided the applicant with performance feedback but he or she thought it was better to take a different approach?"

Sample coachability question to ask your applicants' referees #2

"Could you tell us about a specific time when the applicant was not happy with your directions about an ongoing project?"

Now, imagine you have applicants who are both intrinsically motivated and highly coachable... Yet, there remains one more element to accelerate the learning process—conscientiousness.

Rule 4

Make Sure Your Applicants Are Conscientious Because It is Not Possible to Steer a Parked Car

"With self-discipline most anything is possible."
—Theodore Roosevelt:

In a landmark study, using a representative sample of 9646 adults in the United States, Duckworth et al. showed conscientiousness is the only personality trait linked to both objective and subjective measures of success such as wealth and life satisfaction, respectively.[131]

The study examined the association of each of The Big Five personality traits (not to be confused with our Big Three here)—conscientiousness, openness, extraversion, agreeableness, and emotional stability—and cognitive ability with income, wealth, positive affect, negative affect, and life satisfaction. The results portrayed that only conscientiousness was consistently correlated with all measures of both objective and subjective measures of success. Other traits showed stronger but less consistent associations with the same measures of success. For instance, openness showed negative associations with income, wealth, and life satisfaction. Extraversion showed no correlation with income. Agreeableness showed negative correlations with income, wealth, and life satisfaction. Emotional stability showed little correlation with income and no correlation with wealth. Perhaps the most interesting finding was that although cognitive ability showed a positive correlation with income and wealth, it showed no correlation with positive affect, negative affect, or life satisfaction.

Other studies have corroborated these findings. Poropat et al. showed that conscientiousness is the most reliable predictor of future academic course grades.[132] Roberts et al., Deary et al., and Kern et al. showed that conscientiousness is associated with physical health and longevity.[133–135] Barrick et al. found conscientiousness to be associated with job performance,[136] while Roberts et al. reported it to be most associated with marital stability.[137]

Why is conscientiousness correlated with success?

In order to answer this, we need a precise definition for conscientiousness. While most people know the conventional definition of conscientiousness, every time I ask someone to define it, I get a different response. The responses do not seem to have a definitive framework and are vague at best. Of course, that is not comforting, especially since our goal is to be able to create a reproducible and consistent process. We need a concrete definition to use conscientiousness in the selection process.

The good news is that researchers have already defined conscientiousness. Most focus on 5 domains of conscientiousness—attention to detail, industriousness (tenacious versus lazy), organization (organized versus sloppy), reliability (dependable versus unreliable), and impulse control (cautious versus careless). Given this definition, it is easy to see why conscientious individuals are more successful in all domains of their personal and professional lives, a notion supported by scientific research.

Conscientious individuals act by delaying immediate gratification and focus on long-term results.[138] They avoid unnecessary conflicts and seek to resolve them when these arise.[138] They are more productive—they work hard, remain organized, and make careful decisions.[136] They have more friends as children and, presumably, are better able to tap into the resources of their social networks when they need help.[139,140] Not only that, conscientious individuals enjoy better workplace and social lives; they also tend to be physically healthier[4] and perform better academically.[132]

It is important to note that, as Duckworth et al. explain,[131] the results of their research do not explain whether conscientiousness causes objective and subjective measures of success. Furthermore, most associations have been found to be weak associations. However, the study does have its merits for consideration, since the associations between conscientiousness and measures of success were consistent even after controlling for confounding factors such as the other remaining 4 in the 5 traits examined (openness, extraversion, agreeableness, and emotional stability), cognitive ability, gender, ethnicity, age, and education. Furthermore, the findings have been reproduced by many independent researchers in a variety of settings. My bet is that intrinsic motivation helps people become conscientious; but, in the absence of any empirical evidence, it is best to err on the side of caution and screen applicants for conscientious.

How do you measure conscientiousness?

Believe it or not, you are already measuring some domains of conscientiousness and you do not require a specific tool or question to assess it. But, to make it even more deliberate and systematic, you must train your admissions test evaluators to pay close attention to each domain of conscientiousness. Below, I will highlight specific strategies to assess each domain and provide sample questions.

I. Attention to detail

Think of the last time you sent out an email to a colleague asking 3 questions and received a one-word answer—"yes" or "of course." You naturally had to respond asking them to clarify which question was the response meant to address. In response, they probably said "the first question," in which case you had to email them back *again* asking them to respond to your other questions. In the process, a lot of time would have been wasted and either or both of you probably would have felt frustrated. This example is probably comical; however, it does show the importance of attention to detail, even in trivial non-life-threatening situations.

It is thus clear why attention to detail is essential. Imagine a doctor forgetting a critical diagnostic test or a lawyer missing a court deadline. Even worse, is the fact that individuals with poor attention to detail miss important instructions, consequently leading to frustration, loss of time, productivity, and even significant damages to their organization and those under their care.

The good news is that assessing attention to detail is actually a lot easier than you may think. The following are a few of the strategies we use at SortSmart to assess the attention to detail of applicants.

The most basic strategy to assess attention to detail is embedding a specific keyword or numeric code within your application instruction manual and then asking applicants for that specific information during screening. This works well whether you have a one-page instructional manual on your website or a fifteen-page booklet, although it works best with longer documents. All you should do is include your keyword somewhere halfway or two-thirds of the way in your instructions, asking your applicant to include that keyword in a specific location on their application. The key is *not* to include this information at the beginning or the end of your instructions—most people simply read these parts and skip everything else in between, unless they have excellent attention to detail.

For example, include this in your application manual: "To apply, include [Your code word/number] in the [X section] of your application." For instance, "To apply, include 2035Z after your last name on the application."

You would be surprised to see how many applicants miss this piece of information, which almost always signals a lack of attention to detail, but 1 question is never sufficient to assess any quality.

My favorite method to assess attention to detail is to ask multipart questions during the applicant screening process; if your process is timed—which is absolutely essential (See Rule #6)—you are more likely to find detail-oriented applicants.

Here's a sample question:

"Could you tell us about your past 5 volunteer experiences? Please state the experiences in chronological order starting from the most recent. Please briefly describe your role, the goal of the

organization, the full name of your immediate supervisor, indicating how your supervisor would rate your performance on a scale of 1 to 7, and specify why you left each position."

Imagine having to respond to this question under time pressure right on the spot. It has 7 parts; therefore, it is considerably easier to determine which applicant pays attention to detail under time pressure and stress vs. those that do not.

These types of questions work great when the applicant has to respond in real time, either in a live interview scenario or, even better, in a live-recorded interview with a countdown timer, forcing a quick response without the ability to go back and modify the original response, such as what we do using SortSmart's motivation-based admissions screening software.

The remaining 4 factors of conscientiousness are best assessed with the help of carefully chosen referees, rather than those cherry picked by the applicants (Rule 10); functional tests (Rule 5); or an on-the-spot assessment of past experiences. In the following paragraphs, I will define each factor, providing specific examples.

II. Industriousness

We define industriousness as being hardworking and diligent, as opposed to being lazy. Industrious individuals are more productive and are generally busy following through with the goals they set for themselves and the goals assigned to them as part of their academic life, work, or relationships with others.

Industriousness is best assessed with the help of the applicants' referees. The problem with traditional referees, handpicked by the applicants, is their unreliability and questionable motives. Therefore, I recommend that before you use referees as part of your assessment procedure, you refer to Rule #10, where I discuss exactly how to choose the applicants' referees and how to ask for their input about the applicant in question.

A vital strategy is to avoid explicitly including the adjectives you would like to assess in your questions—even when evaluations are done anonymously, no one wants to be seen or feel like they are negatively evaluating others. The formula for creating questions for referees is the same as that for creating questions for applicants, which I discuss in depth in Rule #13. Note, the sample questions are essentially the same for both the applicants and their referees with subtle differences; this is intentional—it will tell you about the truthfulness of your applicants' responses.

Sample question to ask referees

"Could you tell us about a specific time when you had to provide continuous encouragement to motivate the applicant to take action to complete a project?"

Sample question for applicants

"Could you tell us about a specific time when you needed continuous encouragement to be motivated to complete a project?"

III. Organization

Individuals who are organized can plan in advance; they arrange tasks in their order of priority. They know the value of keeping detailed notes and records. They usually spend a significant amount of time assessing big projects, organizing them into smaller tasks. This generally leads to them being more productive and effective in both work and personal life settings.

Alternately, disorganized individuals are always behind schedule—they forget things, which forces them to have to recreate the same wheel multiple times. They generally do not have a clear plan of action and do what *feels* right instead of what *is* right. They are generally the least productive and take longer to complete tasks and projects. Furthermore, many projects go unfinished or are reassigned.

Sample question to ask referees

"Could you tell us about a specific time when a project assigned to the applicant was delayed due to poor planning and misaligned priorities?"

Sample question to ask applicants

"Could you tell us about a specific time when a project assigned to you was delayed due to poor planning and misaligned priorities?"

IV. Reliability

Reliable individuals are consistent and can be trusted with independent projects within their capabilities without any supervision. They show up on time and they deliver as promised without any surprises.

Unreliable individuals are unpredictable; their work is defined by inconsistency and usually it's hit and miss. They tend to have some sort of excuse such as "my dog ate my cat" or "I had no idea it was going to take this long" or "I'm sorry I totally forget we had a meeting today."

Sample question to ask referees

"Could you tell us about a specific time when you assigned an important project within the applicant's competencies to someone else other than the applicant?"

Sample question to ask applicants

"Could you tell us about a specific time when your supervisor assigned an important project within your competencies to someone else instead of you?"

V. Impulse control

The ability to recognize the importance of long-term thinking and delayed gratification is critical to success in any field. Most fundamental innovations are the result of years and sometimes decades of consistent hard work and dedication led by individuals who sacrifice the joys of everyday life for a better future. At the extreme, such individuals are able to look beyond their own lives and consider the implications of their actions for the betterment of humanity. On the other hand, those who lack impulse control give in to temptations and, as a result, are less productive and cause delays—for example, they may get distracted by a sunny day or a sporting event without realizing the implication of their actions.

Similarly, impulse control is critical in daily interactions with peers. Top-performing professionals can control the urge to respond emotionally in response to the emotions of those under their care. This allows them to build a trusting relationship with others who are more likely to listen to their expertise. Contrarily, practicing professionals lacking impulse control often lose their ability to resist the urge to lash out in response to an unreasonable or angry patient, client, or colleague; this deteriorates their credibility and may even tarnish the reputation of their institutions and professions.

Sample question to ask referees

"Could you tell us about a specific time when you witnessed the applicant prioritizing urgent desires instead of long-term goals?"

"Could you tell us about a time when you witnessed the applicant speak out their mind without intentional deliberation?"

Sample question to ask applicants

"Could you tell us about a specific time when you sacrificed your long-term goals in order to pursue an urgent matter?"

What about other traits such as emotional intelligence, empathy, ethics, and so forth?

These other traits are arguably important; but there are 4 problems with admissions screening practices that are too focused on these types of personality traits instead of focusing on The Big Three. First, most other traits have been shown to correlate with The Big Three and therefore only add complexity to the process. Second, these personality traits are plastic and individuals with the right level of The Big Three can learn all of them. Third, individuals with excellent communications skills and empathy do not necessarily have intrinsic motivation for the job and may not be conscientious or coachable. Lastly, no other trait aside from The Big Three has been shown to correlate with on-the-job behavior or future success; this is not surprising, since such traits can be easily faked during the admissions process by individuals who know how to provide socially acceptable responses to navigate around admissions practices that are too narrowly focused on such traits.

In essence: what good are individuals with remarkable professionalism and outstanding standardized test scores if they are not intrinsically motivated to do their jobs?

You may be asking, "Are you saying we should not assess students for communications skills either?"

I would argue that an individual with remarkable communications skills who is not intrinsically motivated, conscientious, or coachable, will not be a suitable applicant. Such an individual is likely to do a lot of damage to those under their care, their colleagues, and their profession even with excellent communications skills! Conversely, individuals who have the right level of The Big Three will be able to improve their communications skills over time, if they do not already possess such skills. I should add here that nevertheless, in a test such as SortSmart motivation-based admissions screening, where applicants are required to provide both typed and video-recorded responses, verbal and written communications skills are additionally easily assessed, although they are not adequate evaluation criteria on their own.

How about screening for The Big Three and the other traits simultaneously?

Given that the other traits have not been correlated with on-the-job behavior, any additional benefits appear to be insignificant. Furthermore, the process might lead to discrimination against certain applicants from different cultural and socioeconomic backgrounds, as we have seen in Chapter II, with traditional admissions screening practices focusing heavily on such traits. Realistically, it is not possible to accurately and efficiently screen for dozens of traits anyway. Any additional trait adds significant complexity to your entire admissions process. It requires more training for your admissions test evaluators. It requires designing and administrating additional questions. Translation? It requires more time, money, and energy without much added benefits and perhaps even several pitfalls. Remember, our goal is to create the simplest admissions screening protocol that allows you to select top-performing applicants while promoting diversity with less time and cost, rather than further complicating this procedure. Nevertheless, it is important to note that this is an evolving science. It is not perfect. Our mission at SortSmart is to continuously adapt and improve the process based on empirical evidence.

Once you have selected applicants with the right levels of The Big Three, you may want to evaluate their functional competence for the role, a concept examined in the next Rule.

Rule 5

Test the Applicants' Functional Ability

The combination of intrinsic motivation, coachability, and conscientiousness will tell you how applicants are going to behave and perform later during training and, most importantly, in their future jobs as independent professionals. Moreover, they tell you which applicants can quickly learn new skills. However, they do not reveal whether your applicants currently possess any required technical skills. This may not be relevant if you are in charge of screening applicants for professional training, but it is critical if you are screening applicants for professional roles after the completion of formal education and training.

For example, you should not be concerned with clinical skills of premedical students applying to your medical school—if they have a high level of The Big Three, they are going to learn all required clinical skills during their formal training. On the other hand, if you are screening a newly graduated oncologist or a seasoned lawyer for a partnership position, you must test their functional ability *and* The Big Three, since the stakes are high and the expectations are that your applicants for such positions already possess the required technical skills to perform tasks effectively.

Functional tests are used in many high-stake professions. For example, the Objective Structured Clinical Examination (OSCE) is an examination to evaluate the clinical performance of health care professional trainees such as students in medicine, nursing, pharmacy, and dentistry, or a physician's assistant. It is designed to test the students' skills in multiple independent stations, mimicking future real-life scenarios they may face while interacting with patients as practicing professionals. Similarly, law school graduates are normally required to engage in apprenticeships and pass a bar examination that tests their technical skills as future lawyers. Commercial airline pilots are required to have 150–200 hours of supervised flight experience in addition to performing well on functional tests of their knowledge of both flight instruments and navigation. Functional tests are also used in sports. All professional and even most amateur-level sports teams test the technical skills of new team members.

How to test the functional ability of your applicants:

As indicated earlier, if your applicants are applying for professional training, you probably do not require to go beyond testing for The Big Three. This section is most relevant to screening applicants after graduation.

The best way to conduct a functional test is by designing a test that closely mimics *the most important* functional aspect of the future job of your applicants. I emphasize *the most important* because it is not possible to test everything quickly and efficiently; again, if you have tested your applicants for The Big Three, they will learn all other details later, if necessary.

For example, tech giants like Google and Apple, who have become successful largely due to their ability to attract and recruit top talent, test the programming skills of future software developers by requiring the completion of specific work sample tests. During the screening process, programmers are asked to solve technical problems in real time—that is the most important functional aspect of such a role.

The added benefit of functional tests is they can independently reveal more about the conscientiousness and coachability of your applicants. For example, if the applicants pay close attention to the test instructions, you can conclude they are likely conscientious. If they are open to feedback, especially in a collaborative functional test where they are asked to collaborate with other candidates to perform a job-specific technical task, it may be concluded that they are likely coachable.

The following are the general guidelines for designing functional tests:

1. Identify the most important technical aspect of the job and design a test that closely mimics the typical required level of competence for the role.

2. Create detailed instructions for the applicants, such that any applicant of acceptable technical skills (*and* conscientiousness) is able to read the instructions independently and perform the task without the need for clarifying questions or external aid.

3. Ask your entire pool of applicants to take the test.

4. Ask the applicants to perform the task in real time, either under supervision by your interviewers or online as part of the applicant screening process.

5. Assign a numeric score (see Rule #7) to the functional test responses.

6. Restrict the response time. This allows you to both standardize the process across all applicants and get a sense of their ability to function under real-world pressures like deadlines. In fact, your entire screening process must be timed, which brings us to our next Rule.

Rule 6

Use a Timed Screening Process to Facilitate Genuine Responses

Whether you are assessing your applicants for The Big Three, testing their functional ability, or gathering more information from their referees, you should always use a timed screening process—yes, even for your applicants' referees.

Setting time limits ensures the applicants (and referees) are thinking on the spot and not researching and tailoring their answers. This helps facilitate genuine responses,[141] especially since we focus on questions constructed in relation to specific past experiences, rather than hypothetical situations.

The most efficient and cost-effective way to achieve this is using an online software. For example, SortSmart's software is designed to impose a time restriction per question. As applicants review each question, they see a countdown timer that restricts their response to a specific amount of time. Once the timer reaches zero, the applicants are automatically taken to the next question; they are not able to pause the test or go back to make any changes to their response. This process continues until the test is completed, which takes roughly 60 minutes from start to finish. We choose sufficient amount of time to ensure that applicants have the necessary time to formulate their response, but not enough time to start calling friends or searching the web for socially acceptable responses, although this would be extremely difficult, as all of our questions are specifically designed to describe certain past experiences.

Aside from obvious benefits, there is a hidden advantage in using a timed screening process. It makes the entire process fair and promotes diversity, treating all applicants equally. In a traditional applicant screening process, applicants are asked to submit their applications at a specific deadline and are given months, usually during spring and summer, before the application deadline to complete their personal statements, letters of recommendations, and so forth. Here, those from lower income families are at a clear disadvantage, not possessing the luxury of time. They are likely working part-time, if not full-time, to pay their bills and maybe even supporting their families, whereas their wealthier counterparts can take the entire summer off to work on their applications *and* have them edited multiple times by a wealthy support group likely familiar with the admissions process and having time to assert their support. On the other hand, during a timed admissions process, every applicant, regardless of socioeconomic status, race, gender, or cultural background, gets an equal opportunity to participate.

A timed screening process can help prompt applicants in providing genuine responses, however, you also require a strategy for assigning a numeric score to each response to make the evaluation quantitative and scientific. We will discuss numeric scoring next.

Rule 7

Use a Numeric Scoring System

The overall goal of your admissions process is to distinguish suitable versus unsuitable applicants. The best and perhaps the only way to achieve this is by assigning a numeric score to each applicant. This allows for a systematic, high resolution, and defensible discernment, as compared to resorting to gut feeling or "yes/no" or "agree/disagree" type of scoring systems. Working with the resulting quantitative data allows one to draw conclusions, reports, results, and graphs from responses.

Importantly, you must apply an independent, robust numeric scoring system to each part of your admissions process. For example, you must assess each of the 3 parts of your admissions process—The Big Three, functional tests, and referees' responses—using a numeric scoring system, in addition to anything else that you may want to take into consideration. Incidentally, such a strategy will help reduce implicit bias, if used correctly in combination with the other strategies in this book, because it forces the evaluators to remain objective.

How to design a robust numeric scoring scale.

The best scoring scale is a 7-point Likert scale, rather than a 5-point scale, a 9-point scale, or any form of an even-numbered scale. In fact, I have intentionally chosen to discuss numeric scoring as "Rule #7" hoping that the repetition and association will help you remember this very important detail for reasons explained below.

First, it is important to note that your numeric scoring scale should include an odd number of choices—even-numbered scales do not include a middle ground or a neutral point. This does not allow your evaluators to choose a point of neutrality and forces all scores to either extreme, reducing the validity and reliability.

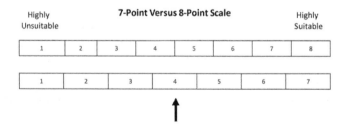

Figure 18. Odd-numbered scales are considered more favorable because they offer a point of neutrality or mid point (indicated by the arrow).

In a set of office hardware and application system usability studies, Lewis asked office workers to rate their satisfaction with the use of a printer, a word processor, a mail application, a calendar application, and a spreadsheet. He found that the mean differences correlated more strongly with observed significant levels of t-tests when using 7-point scales, as compared to 5-point scales.[142]

Preston and Colman studied the reliability, validity, and discriminating power of scales of differing response categories, where participants were asked to rate service elements associated with a recently visited restaurant or store. The study showed that reliability, validity, and the discriminating power of the scales significantly increased up to approximately 7-point scales and tended to decrease for scales with over 10 response categories. Notably, the difference between the 7-point and 9-point scales were miniscule, with minor added benefits if any.[143]

Finstad, in a series of usability tests on 2 software applications using 172 Intel employees, showed that the 5-point scale is less sensitive to capture the true range of responses from participants, eliciting more interpolations, as compared to the 7-point Likert scale. Consequently, the 5-point scales resulted in inaccurate measures of true responses by participants, making participants more likely to violate defined boundaries.[144]

It is thus favorable to use a 7-point scale, owed to its acceptable sensitivity, validity, and reliability. A 9-point scale on the other hand has minor benefits, if any, over a 7-point scale; it is likely to confuse your test evaluators and lead to unnecessary inefficiencies due to increased decision time taken by evaluators.

Labeling the 7-point scale appropriately is equally critical; care must be taken to avoid a common pitfall. Researchers often label every single response category to force an appropriate response from each participant. However, this practice might lead to biased responses in applicant screening, since the label for each category assigns an adjective to your applicants. This might make some of your evaluators to generally choose gentler adjectives as they may be inclined to avoid being too harsh to applicants, while others might most often assign harsher adjectives. It is easy to understand why this could be problematic in applicant screening by skewing responses to one extreme or the other, significantly impeding your ability to discern the best-suited applicants. Therefore, a better solution is to only label the 2 extremes of your scales to allow your admissions test evaluators to select each of the items in between them, at their discretion, while being instructed to use the entire scale when comparing applicants.

The subsequent figure shows how you can label a 7-point Likert scale.

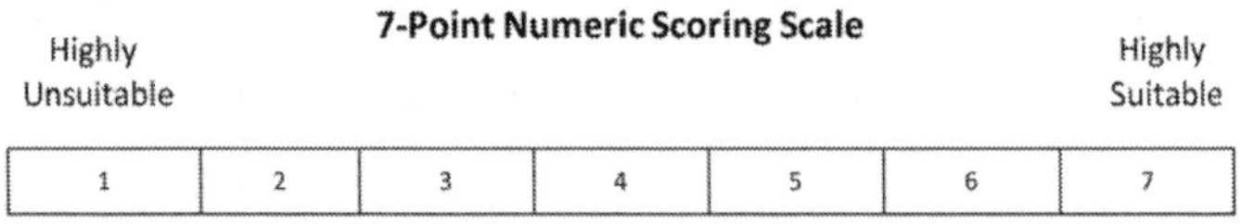

7-Point Numeric Scoring Scale

Highly Unsuitable						Highly Suitable
1	2	3	4	5	6	7

Figure 19. The 7-point scale labeled at each extreme end.

In addition to choosing the right scoring strategy, another method can considerably increase the reliability of your admissions screening process, which includes the use of multiple independent evaluators, as discussed in Rule 8.

Rule 8

Utilize a Group of Independent Trained Evaluators to Increase the Reliability of Your Admissions Screening and Reduce Implicit Bias

Before we discuss the importance of using multiple independent evaluators for the admissions process, we need to define test reliability.

Test reliability refers to the ability of a test to produce similar and stable results under consistent conditions. For example, a ruler is said to be reliable if it shows the same measurement of length for letter size paper, whether the measurement is made today or a month from now, if all conditions such as temperature, atmospheric pressure, and so forth remain consistent. A ruler is unreliable if every time the same object is measured, it shows a different length, under the same conditions.

Reliability of a test is typically measured in multiple ways: internal consistency, inter-rater reliability, parallel forms reliability, and test-retest reliability, all of which are critical and should be examined before the test is administered.[145,146]

Internal consistency refers to the measure of similarity between different questions that examine the same construct. For example, 2 questions designed to measure the truthfulness of applicants should result in similar results, for the test to be considered to have high internal consistency.

Inter-rater reliability is the degree to which examinations by independent evaluators produces similar results for the same set of questions. A test is said to have high inter-rater reliability if there is a significant consensus amongst independent evaluators marking the same test for the same applicants.

Parallel forms reliability is a measure of correlation between different versions of the same test; it examines the same constructs administered to the same group of applicants within a short period of time under the same conditions. If a test has high parallel form reliability, different versions of the test produces similar results for the same group of applicants.

Test-retest reliability refers to the measure of correlation between the same test administered to the same group of applicants within a short period of time.

There are several ways to increase test reliability while reducing implicit bias.

1. Use of multiple questions to assess the same constructs. Normally, you would need 4–6 questions per construct; in fact, we use a total of 15 questions at SortSmart to assess The Big Three.

2. Applicants must take the test under consistent conditions. This includes familiarity with the test and the user interface, in addition to controlling for the date and time of day. Furthermore, the applicants should take the test in similar environments. For example, with SortSmart, applicants can take a sample test to become familiar with the software's interface and question types. Additionally, we are able to schedule tests for each program to be taken at the same time and date and ask applicants to take the test in a quiet room with a closed door, so they are not interrupted during the test. Importantly, the entire test is timed, and applicants have a specific amount of time to answer each question.

3. Questions for each measured construct must be carefully designed to ensure they are free of cultural, gender-based, racial, or socioeconomic bias, in addition to the ability to measure the desired criterion.

4. Regular testing of measures of reliability and the removal of unreliable questions.

5. Use of multiple independent trained evaluators who are blind to the applicants' identity.

The last point is the hardest to implement and yet the most important way to increase reliability of any admissions test. It merits additional explanation because, incidentally, it can also promote diversity if done correctly.

Bias can infiltrate and undermine many parts of the applicant screening process and remains a great concern. For example, studies have demonstrated that a male name is significantly more likely to receive an interview call or an offer than an identical application bearing a female name.[147] An English-sounding name is more likely to receive an interview than one that sounds ethnic.[148] Any in-person interview that follows the initial written application process usually exacerbates this problem. Here, in addition to gender, the interviewer may be biased by background, physical appearance, body posture, or manner of speaking. Science consistently shows that interviewers are subconsciously drawn to the applicants most like themselves. The overall negative effect is that bias can narrow your talent pool and not enough applicants are fairly and adequately screened because of the time and cost required to conduct in-person interviews for the entire applicant pool. In this way, perfect applicants may be missed by your admissions screening process. There are several strategies that can help reduce bias.

The first step in evaluating admissions test results is to ensure the examiners are highly trained to know exactly how to grade each question. This includes training each evaluator about the logistics of the test and the desired evaluation criteria followed by a *functional* examination of their performance to ensure only highly-competent individuals are allowed to act as evaluators.

Second, evaluators must be from a diverse group of individuals representing varying cultural, racial, and socioeconomic status and the evaluators should also have an equal male to female ratio to avoid gender bias. Furthermore, each question for each applicant must be evaluated by an independent evaluator blind to personal identifiers and the performance of the applicant on other parts of the same test and in other parts of the admissions process.

Assuming that you will be using an online screening software, a sound procedure to ensure your evaluators are blind to the applicant's identity is to filter any video and voice recordings so that the evaluators experience all applicants as being similar in visual and audio representation. This practice virtually eliminates any implicit cultural and racial bias, because the evaluator cannot see the applicants, nor can they discern each applicant's subtle accents.

In this way, the use of a diverse group of evaluators who are carefully trained not only increases test reliability, but also promotes diversity by compensating for each individual's implicit bias to ensure that no applicant is treated unfairly.

In the near future, reliability will be greatly enhanced and implicit bias will be virtually eliminated with the help of artificial intelligence. But until then, the above strategy will be an order of magnitude improvement over traditional applicant screening.

While test reliability is essential, it is not sufficient on its own. For a test to be useful in the admissions process—or in any context for that matter—it must also be a valid measure of the criteria it is intended to measure. Going back to our ruler example, a ruler could be said to be reliable if it consistently indicates the same length for the same object under the same conditions. However, if it consistently adds 2 cm to the true length of any object, while this shows reliability, it is not a valid measure of length. This brings us to test validity, discussed in the next section.

Rule 9

Use a Test with High Predictive Validity for Future Behaviors and Avoid the Trap of "Tests of Tests"

Test validity refers to the ability of a test to measure what it is designed to measure. It can be broken down into 3 categories: construct validity, content validity, and criterion validity.[149,150]

Construct validity refers to the degree to which a test can measure intended constructs. For example, a ruler is a valid tool for measuring distance, but is not a valid test for measuring the temperature of a room.

Content validity is a measure of how well a test can assess all elements of a construct. For example, an admissions test for testing suitability of future medical doctors might only assess the applicants' ability to memorize facts, such as what is observed for certain sections of the MCAT, and thus be unable to measure whether the applicants have genuine motivation to pursue medicine, their coachability, and their conscientiousness.

Criterion validity is the ability of a test to predict desired outcomes and can be divided into concurrent and predictive validity. Concurrent validity is the degree to which the test can predict an outcome measured at the same time as the test. For example, if performance on a practical clinical skills test correlates with performance on a written clinical skills test that has been taken at the same time, the 2 tests are said to have concurrent validity. Predictive validity refers to the ability of a test to predict an outcome measured in the future. For example, if performance on an admissions tests can predict future on-the-job behavior, the test is said to have predictive validity.

Predictive validity is the ultimate goal of any admissions test. While some admissions screening tools such as grades, standardized tests (for example, MCAT, LSAT, SAT, etc.), and situational judgment tests have shown varying degrees of predictive validity for future *tests*, none have demonstrated convincingly predictive validity for future on-the-job behavior because they do not measure appropriate indicators of future behavior, including The Big Three attributes. Incidentally, this indicates that traditional admissions screening tools also lack construct and content validity. In fact, a close examination reveals that most traditional admissions screening tools are merely a test of a test!

This is how we realized early on during the development of the SortSmart test that we had to focus on specific predictors of future behavior, which led us to choose intrinsic motivation, conscientiousness, and coachability.

On the other hand, most other admissions tests are designed to correlate with future tests and by default are largely flawed.

To overcome this limitation, it is critical to measure the degree of correlation of the test with The Big Three instead. This simple mind shift will result in creation of an admissions screening test that has superior predictive validity compared to traditional practices.

There is one additional method that should theoretically increase the validity of an admissions test, which in practice is normally found to be ineffective and often detrimental. In Rule 10, we will examine a new way to utilize the help of applicants' referees that may actually help your admissions process.

Rule 10

Choose the Applicants' References Wisely

Traditional methods of obtaining references are largely unreliable and ineffective. There is no empirical evidence to support the reliability of referees during the selection process. The applicant can simply select their best references (usually 3). If the applicants have varied experiences, asking for a very small sample will not provide an adequate assessment. This allows the applicants to shape the narrative of their professional career; it can be no more trustworthy than the personal statements, as discussed earlier. Even worse, the identity of the referees is rarely confirmed and it is often difficult to do so. Moreover, references obtained in this way can cause further bias, since applicants from a higher socioeconomic status have a broader network of friends and family, with influencers to act as their referees; alternatively, they might have learned how to engineer their behavior to seek references from top influencers. In this way, it is best to not use references at all, unless they are obtained differently.

Below, I have highlighted the 6 steps required to use references in a meaningful way while further reducing implicit bias.

1. You must choose the referees yourself, instead of allowing the applicant to cherry pick the list of referees. A more sophisticated admissions process could involve asking for a chronological list of individuals who have acted as supervisors, bosses, or colleagues and randomly sampling a number to contact. Another strategy would be for your admissions team to ask to speak with specific past supervisors or colleagues who have come up during the selection process, specifically individuals brought up during the admissions test. If the applicant is reluctant to provide the details of specific individuals, it is normally a red flag that must be investigated further before making any admission decision.

2. The minimum number of references required to get an adequate sample should be 5 independent individuals, and not the default of 3.

3. Referees should be asked to assess The Big Three using questions that indirectly assess each quality. I have provided several sample questions to be asked of referees in the previous sections, on intrinsic motivation, conscientiousness, and coachability.

4. The responses provided by the referees must be numerically scored using the same scoring system utilized for evaluating applicants' responses. The

final score can provide yet another robust and quantitative decision-making tool.

5. The identify of each referee must be verified seamlessly. The use of video-based responses ensures that their identity is verifiable when used in combination with ID detection technology.

6. The entire process must take place online, to ensure it is efficient and scalable for use by all applicants.

While traditional reference checks may not be beneficial to the admissions screening process, the above steps not only help select better applicants but can help promote diversity by leveling the playing field.

However, what if the applicant scores well on all tested criteria and yet, it turns out that your program is just a back-up for them? No admissions screening will be perfect. Yet, there exist certain ways to reduce the number of back-up seekers, as we will discuss next.

Rule 11

Identify the "Back-Up" Seekers to Prevent Costly Turnovers

Most applicants are guilty of having positions that they apply simply as a "back up" to their ideal choice. Applicant turnover is expensive—the effect of losing a superstar, someone with high potential or someone trained and doing an important job well, can leave an impact on both team morale and the institution. The costs included in replacing an applicant are as follows: cost of screening and selecting a new person (advertising, interviewing, and screening); lost productivity (the new person could take years to reach the productivity of the existing person); lost engagement (high turnover could lead to disengagement of other members of the profession); increased error rate (new applicants will lack specific problem solving skills); training cost, and cultural impact (when one applicant leaves, others will undoubtedly wonder "why?").

It is thus essential to recognize applicants who are at high risk for voluntary departure. If done correctly, this can be concluded with pointed questions during the selection process. Your admissions committee must look for the level of specificity, language use, and passion in the applicant's response. How much does the applicant seem to be invested in this admissions test? What do they know about your institution? How much research has this person done in preparation for this admissions test? Do they have any insight into your culture, mission, or core values that signifies some reflection on their part? These are some questions that your admissions committee must consider when analyzing each applicant's response.

While this is challenging and it might not always be possible to pinpoint who is genuinely interested versus those who may be faking it to secure a backup plan and buy themselves time, the use of intrinsic motivation in the screening process normally eliminates such applicants. However, some might be genuinely interested in the profession, but might be considering your institution as a backup. Therefore, you need a strategy to look out for these applicants, carefully analyzing their responses and that of their referees.

Earlier, I cited this question as a means of assessing intrinsic motivation: "If you are not accepted this year, what are your backup plans?" The goal was to find out whether the applicants were going to reveal any backup plans related to their chosen profession. But what if *your* program is their backup plan? How will you find that out?

While we have collected considerable data about this issue, both from hiring practices and admissions screening of university applicants, it remains a difficult question to answer. Nevertheless, I will share our experience below.

The first clue comes from the applicants' response to the question. If this is not related to the program or the profession, then, not only may they be extrinsically motivated, but additionally, your program may be their second choice. As always, it is best to ask a variety of questions and get help from the applicants' referees before coming to a decision.

Furthermore, there exists another way to tell if some applicants are backup seekers or not. The best approach appears to be by judging the applicants' actions after an offer of admission has been granted or is about to be offered.

Here are some other common red flags:

The applicants' response to whether they are willing to sign the necessary documents and pay initial tuition costs, if they are offered a position within the next few days or weeks, is vague. It is not a clear "yes." Instead, backup seekers are usually not as enthusiastic as genuine applicants; they "need time to think about it."

The applicant is late to respond to any queries after the offer of admission or is always responding close to the deadline.

The applicant does not have any questions about a brand-new experience and is not proactively seeking clarifications about the program details.

While I may risk repeating myself, it is critical to point out that the above are generalizations; applicants might have legitimate reasons for wanting to deliberate or responding late—this is why I continue to emphasize that your admissions team must examine their behavior from multiple angles, hence the need to design at least 4 to 5 questions for each attribute to be tested.

I believe the point here is best illustrated using an example; I will provide an example from one of my friends who is the cofounder of a high growth start-up—we will call my friend "Ben" and his company "Startup Inc."—which will provide clear parallels in the admissions screening process, especially for more senior roles such as medical residency or post-doctoral positions.

Several years ago, Startup Inc. had an employee—we will call him "Jim"—working as a part-time junior scientist. When Jim joined their team, he was already fully employed elsewhere. After about a year, Jim asked Ben if it would be possible to transition to full-time, which prompted Ben to ask him about his full-time position. Jim then explained that his work was under a non-renewable contract and that he had decided to come work with Startup Inc. instead, because he enjoyed his work. So far, so good. Since Startup Inc. was already looking to hire someone with his skills, this made perfect sense for both parties. It seemed like a win-win. Ben asked Jim to set up a time to speak about his possible future roles; Jim agreed to get in touch. Several weeks passed, and since Ben had not heard anything, he followed up—they eventually set up a time to meet. This was already a red flag for Ben. He rationalized that if Jim is genuinely interested in the position and is about to lose his full-time job, he should be eager to organize his future.

Nevertheless, Ben decided to continue the conversation. During their meeting, they came to an agreement including salary, work hours, roles, and responsibilities. Ben asked Jim to send him an email with the bullet points of their agreement, so that he could draft a formal employment agreement. Jim agreed enthusiastically. Again, weeks passed, and Ben did not hear back. This was the second red flag—he could not ignore it this time. Instead, Ben had a meeting with his management team to see if they had noticed anything odd. Since Jim was seemingly very agreeable, nobody had noticed anything unusual. But Ben was still not convinced;

so, he set up another meeting with Jim to discuss this issue further.

Jim's response was that he was trying to plan the start date and coordinate with his wife before getting back to Ben, since she had secured a faculty position that would require relocation. The relocation would not affect their working relationship, since Jim's role was remote, but it would require him to take time off to move the family. This explanation seemed to make sense; so, Ben asked Jim to get back to him with a concrete date. Eventually, Jim got back to Ben with a firm date and Ben produced a formal agreement for him to sign. This is when another distinct red flag appeared. Ben had given Jim a week to sign the agreement; but, 10 days passed and, again, he did not hear back from Jim. Eventually Ben received an email from Jim citing a list of excuses why he might not be able start at their agreed-upon date and thus why he was not comfortable signing their agreement. To cut a long story short, it eventually became clear that the position Jim was seeking with Startup Inc. was his backup, in case the relocation plans did not work out as planned. The minute Jim's wife and the rest of the family were granted a visa to relocate, Jim quit and was not even interested in working part-time anymore. Of course, Ben was not interested in him continuing part-time either, given the months of delay in their hiring process and Jim's lack of integrity.

In hindsight, it was clear that something had been wrong from day one. There were many warning signs; but, because on the surface Jim seemed like a really nice guy, they had ignored the warning signs, wasting a lot of time and money in the process. Here is the real kicker. It turned out Jim was not nice at all, because after his departure, during a Startup Inc. post-mortem meeting, they discovered that his wife had completed his functional test when he had originally applied to work with them as part-time staff! The sad news was that Jim had forgotten to remove his wife's name and comments from the document he had submitted with his application; even worse was the fact that the Startup Inc. HR staff member who had originally examined this document had not noticed this very obvious red flag, which should have eliminated Jim from their applicant pool before even being considered for an interview. Incidentally, they realized that specific HR team member had been fired shortly after they had hired Jim due to lack of conscientiousness!

Rule 12

Use a Test with Robust Security Features

A common question from new, prospective SortSmart partners, which normally include program admissions deans or directors, is whether or not the test is secure to ensure applicants are unable to cheat during the test. This is a really good question, since most admissions professionals know that the traditional applicant screening methods such as personal statements are not verifiable. In fact, it would not be too shocking to discover applicants' parents wrote their personal statement for them. This is even more important in an online test taken by applicants in a location of their own choosing.

There are several methods you can use to increase test security; we employ some simple tactics vs. several proprietary strategies to ensure test security. I will disclose several of our simple tactics here.

The most obvious way to increase test security is employing proctors; you may think this is futile if you are doing this online and screening your entire pool of applicants. It turns out that not only is this feasible, but effective and relatively inexpensive to ensure test security when using an appropriate online test. During SortSmart tests, applicants are continuously monitored via their computer's video camera and microphone; we verify that both work at all times. Furthermore, our test evaluators are trained to flag any response that might include an instance of cheating in the form of third-party presence, since at least half of the applicant responses are video recorded during tests. Moreover, our security team conducts thorough random checks of applicants to include a third layer of security. This makes our tests more secure than an in-person, proctored exam.

Furthermore, every applicant's ID is checked prior to taking the test and verified to match the applicant who is actually present throughout the entire test. These 2 strategies and 8 other proprietary strategies and tools make our tests virtually cheat proof. I highly recommend that you employ some of these strategies for your admissions process if you choose to create your own software.

While we have already discussed 12 critical Rules for admissions screening, there is one more Rule crucial to your admissions process: Designing questions that select the best, while promoting diversity.

Rule 13

Design Questions That Select the Best While Promoting Diversity

I have found 9 key strategies that work best when designing questions. The principal questions for consideration are as follows: What are the main characteristics of a good question? What should a good question accomplish? What should a good question avoid?

Top 3 characteristics of any carefully designed admissions screening question are listed below:

1. It should force applicants to tell the truth, rather than a fabricated, socially accepted response.

2. It should promote diversity by being equally accessible to applicants of varying gender, cultural, racial, and socioeconomic backgrounds.

3. It should allow one to discern poor versus excellent responses, using a numeric scoring scale.

The following is the SortSmart formula for designing questions with all these characteristics:

1: Avoid hypothetical questions.

Hypothetical questions not only cause bias, as we saw earlier, but are problematic as they lead applicants to provide a socially acceptable response, making them a poor choice for accurate candidate selection. Consequently, in my opinion, situational judgment tests have been shown to cause bias and are not correlated with on-the-job behavior because of heavy emphasis on hypothetical questions.

Here is an example of a common hypothetical question: "<u>If</u> you were in a study group and two group members approached you saying that they are upset with a third group member who is not contributing as much, what would you do?"

This is a poor question, since it does not ask for a specific past experience; rather, it throws the applicant into a hypothetical social example and the applicant is immediately able to tell that the question is asking for the most socially acceptable response. The best way to remember this concept is to avoid questions starting with "if" statements. This is true for almost all circumstances, with few exceptions, as we will see shortly.

2: Avoid leading questions.

Many common questions are leading questions. For example, "Describe a time when you came into conflict with an authority figure and <u>how you coped with it</u>" or

"When dealing with multiple demands, <u>how do you set priorities to manage your time?</u>"

These are probably some of the worst questions to ask, since they lead the applicant to ponder a coping strategy to manage their time by setting priorities. In essence, such questions already give away the socially acceptable responses. They do not allow you to discern who is telling the truth. Instead, they can only provide an impression of who is better at formulating socially acceptable responses. Not surprisingly, applicants from higher socioeconomic backgrounds and, especially, extroverted individuals do much better on such questions; yet sadly, they are not necessarily the best applicants and this process introduces inadvertent bias in the admissions process.

3: Ask questions requiring a specific past example.

If you cannot ask hypothetical questions and leading questions, then what is left? I am glad you asked.

Almost all questions asked, with the exception of some that directly assess the level of intrinsic motivation, should be designed to seek an understanding of the applicant in the context of their past experiences, without leading them into providing a socially acceptable response.

Here is an example: "Could you tell us about a <u>specific example</u> when you came into conflict with an authority figure?"

Did you notice what I did there? I used our example from the last section and simply removed the "how you coped with it" part, thus changing the sentence to ask for a *specific* example. Moreover, I turned it into a question that is personable, rather than a dry statement. Now, the applicant is forced to think about a *specific* past experience. If their answer includes a specific name, you also have one potential real reference, who you can ask to speak to if the applicant advances in your admissions process.

This is still not my favorite question. It is a common question and you may run into a canned response that sounds genuine. However, I chose this as an example, since it illustrates the current consideration well. In the next section, I will show you how to turn this question from good to fantastic.

Pro tip: As we have discussed earlier, you should keep an eye out for potential references, at all times. Your goal is to find people who the applicant might not necessarily want you to speak to, since these individuals usually provide the best insights about the applicant's true personality. Furthermore, I showed you how to automate and anonymize the process earlier to ensure it can be done at scale and without the referees' fear of consequences.

4: Ask leading questions.

"Wait. What? Behrouz, you just said 'Avoid leading questions'!"

I know. I know. Well, this is a different kind of leading question that actually works in your favor. It is completely acceptable, and even desirable, to ask questions that lead the applicants in unexpected ways. I have found that this is one of the best ways to get to the truth quickly.

Consider this example:

"Could you tell us about a specific time when your boss or supervisor provided you with criticism about your performance, but you thought it was better to take a different approach?"

This is essentially the same question as "Could you tell us about a specific example when you came into conflict with an authority figure?" However it is better, since it does not say "conflict," which is implied, and leads the applicant to admit that they did not simply abide by the rules blindly all the time by stating "but you thought it was better to take a different approach."

In my experience, this question can reveal a wealth of information about the applicant. First, it forces the applicant to provide a specific instance and, almost always, the name of the supervisor and their role comes up, especially in responses provided by suitable applicants (I'll explain why unsuitable applicants normally provide vague answers in Chapter V). Second, you will have an opportunity to examine exactly how this applicant takes criticism, which allows you to assess coachability. Third, you can assess their conflict resolution capabilities. This question kills 3 birds with one stone—this is exactly what you want in high-stakes admissions. You do not get a second chance to assess the applicants' suitability, so each question must be designed to cover multiple angles.

5: Ask questions that allow you to assign a range of numeric scores.

Every question you ask must allow you to assign a numeric score to each response. In Rule #7, we talked about choosing a 7-point scale instead of a 5-point or 9-point scale, or even worse, an even numbered scale. This is critical, because if you cannot assign a numeric score for each response, you are relying on a "gut feeling" instead of objective, systematic, and scientific admissions screening.

With this consideration, every time you create a new question, ask yourself whether it would be possible for your evaluators to assign a numeric score for each response. It is best to illustrate this by studying a few examples.

This is an example of a question that is *not* going to allow you to assign a range of numeric scores:

"Tell me about yourself."

How will you choose who gets a 2/7 and who gets a 6/7? Who gets a 3/7? What about a 5/7? It is clearly not possible to assign a numeric score in a meaningful way because the question is extremely broad. It is also not really a question. Rather it is a directive statement that does not make the applicants feel comfortable. I would argue that this has to be one of the worst questions to ask not just because you will not be able to assign a numeric score, but also because it is a very common question in every educational program and industry. Questions like these are only going to tell you about the red flags, but will not allow you to devise a systematic approach to assign a range of numeric scores.

Allow me to explain further. Let us assume that some applicants indicate that they come from an immigrant family and they had nothing when they arrived. They struggled to get used to the culture and learn the language, and they pursued education and in fact they represent the first person who attended university in their family. They tell you how hard they had to work to pay for education on their own by working a job and a half while also attending school full time. They tell you that they learned x, y, or z attributes by working as a cashier and later at a fast food restaurant. That could represent a vast number of individuals. How will you assign a numeric score to each applicant?

However, real life is even more complicated. Let us assume that some of the other applicants explain that they are 5 generation natives. They were inspired because they had several doctors, lawyers, dentists, and teachers in the family who mentored them. As a result, they got to travel extensively, learned to play the piano and played in some major event, played in their school's varsity basketball team where they helped win two championships, and even built homes for the homeless in the summer of their first year of undergraduate studies. How will you distinguish between these types of responses? How do you assign a numeric score between this group of applicants vs. the first group of applicants?

The sad truth is that we are usually biased to pick the second group as the group with the strongest response to this question, which leads to inadvertent bias.

Does it make sense to assign a numeric score based on the applicants' upbringing? Can we judge people based on where they came from? Absolutely not, because nobody has a choice about their family, culture, race, and even childhood/early adulthood experiences. Those are a function of the lottery of life. We cannot decide which family, experiences, and/or socioeconomic environment we are born into, and we cannot easily change our environment, at least not until later in life. We certainly cannot decide our cultural or racial experiences. Then why ask a question that gets most, if not all applicants to tell us about such considerations? Worst of all this question does not tell you anything about the applicants' level of intrinsic motivation, conscientiousness, or coachability.

6: Catch bees with honey not vinegar.

Every question you ask must make the applicants feel comfortable because when applicants feel comfortable, they are more likely to open up and tell the truth. This is another reason why "Tell me about yourself" is not a valuable question. It is not even a question rather it is a statement that sounds like an order. Orders and directives will instead make people feel tense, closed, and acutely aware that they are being judged. Their primal brain goes into high fight-or-flight response mode and they will be defensive. They will dig deep for the best socially acceptable response and may not tell you the truth.

Instead, help the applicants to feel more comfortable. Make them feel that you truly care to get to know them and, in the process, give yourself permission to be a little vulnerable. Remember, you are looking for needles in haystacks and top performers have choice and they know it. They tend to gravitate toward environments that are going to help them grow. They are attracted to climates that support their desire for autonomy, relatedness, and optimal challenge. All essential elements that sustain and grow their intrinsic motivation. The slightest hint that your institution is going to be too overbearing and authoritative will force them to run away.

Instead of giving orders as your first impression, ask genuine questions—ask these in a friendly tone. This does not mean you have to compromise the integrity of your admissions process or look "weak" in the eyes of your applicants. In fact, I believe with the right line of questioning you will actually look confident and establish your authority while being supportive, genuine, and caring. We have already seen this in the examples I provided. Most of our questions start with "Would you tell us…" or "Could you tell us…"—they ensure that you are asking a question instead of accidentally giving an order. They are more pleasant to your applicants' ears and it gets them to lower their guards.

7: Mix it up.

I recommend that you develop at least 10 variations of the questions you intend to utilize to assess intrinsic motivation, conscientiousness, and coachability. For example, if you are asking 15 questions during your selection process, you must have 150 questions ready. The process may not be quick, especially since you may not be used to developing questions using the new strategies learned in this book; however, I assure it will be well worth the effort. Having multiple sets of questions allows your team to change the questions for each admissions cycle to prevent your applicants from discerning a pattern or getting used to your questions.

8: Build redundancy.

One of the best strategies you can use to increase the reliability of your admissions screening is by creating redundancy. Our goal is to assess the level of each of The Big Three through *multiple* questions targeting each trait. This is important for several reasons. First, your applicants are less likely to pick up on the patterns and provide you with socially acceptable responses and are more likely to tell you the truth about themselves. Second, when you build redundancy, you introduce fail-safe mechanisms in your admissions process. If any issues arise and a few questions are missed, you will still have other questions that assess The Big Three. You are less likely to suffer from common issues that can negatively impact your admissions process such as technical issues, unreasonable graders, and the law of small numbers. The more questions you ask, the more likely you are to uncover the truth about each applicant.

9: Test, test, test and then repeat.

While it is rare to create optimal questions at the onset, it is feasible to find ideal questions using continuous trial and error. Testing new questions against your original archive of questions is by far the best and fastest way to create a collection of high-performing questions. We are normally testing 2–3 questions at all times. This allows us to continuously refine our questions based on how applicants respond and how our evaluators score their responses. Moreover, we use the feedback received from our evaluators by carefully reviewing their comments.

Keep in mind that whenever you are testing questions—which should be all the time—you should keep both your applicants and your graders in the dark to avoid confounding variables. Of course, while this is clear, please follow your local ethical standards and laws at all times.

The procedures we have discussed to this point will help you create an admissions process that is fair to applicants, selects best-suited individuals, and promotes diversity. However, it is not possible to implement these approaches without the right policies, which brings us to Rule #14.

Rule 14

Democratize the Admissions Process and Educational Institutions

When I speak to admissions deans and directors, it is clear that there are 2 types of institutions out there—ones that are innovative and have no time for red tape and those whose progress stagnates owed to the fear of the unknown and the comfort in existing situations. The first group normally contacts us and starts inquiring about how to take advantage of our services immediately. We normally do not even need to convince them of the benefits of using our system. However, the second group often complains that they want to see changes quickly, but their hands are tied by their institutions' bureaucracy and various stakeholders who want to hang on to the status quo for several reasons. Incidentally, they all agree that we must remain cognizant that admissions practices and tools developed in the past, while likely well-intentioned, are subject to continuous learning and improvement over time as any body of knowledge—this is the essence of self-improvement as a society. Furthermore, they agree that while the status quo is comforting, it is also an impediment to progress and growth.

One of our greatest achievements as human beings is our ability to form social groups to cooperate toward common goals. The introduction of democracy has greatly enhanced this process. The principles of democracy seek to ensure that every qualified individual has the ability to run for leadership positions within different branches of the government, while every member of the public is allowed to have a direct say in who can or cannot assume such leadership roles. Furthermore, the implementation of democratically-elected governing bodies ensures that the leaders' decisions are constantly challenged to reach the most beneficial conclusions that serve the society well, while minimizing harm, oversights, and conflicts of interest.

The same model can be applied to universities and colleges to introduce positive change and remove unnecessary red tape. While its implementation may at first face resistance and be riddled with setbacks and challenges, the benefits outweigh these initial difficulties. Based on historical evidence in other areas, democratically-elected admissions personnel, including admissions deans, directors, officers, and committee members, are more likely to do what is best for the overall good of their institutions, their applicants, and society as a whole, rather than those appointed to such positions without a democratic election process. In case of a democratic election, the possibility of members of the public terminating such positions ensures that the staff stays accountable. Furthermore, by limiting the term of service for such positions, institutions can ensure a continuous stream of fresh ideas and constant change, both of which are essential for improvement and innovation. Notably, with the advent of technology and the use of secure online voting systems, the entire election process can be made more efficient and cost effective. Ultimately, one can argue that it is at least worth testing such policy changes before being succumbed by the fear of the unknown.

While by no means comprehensive, here are some ideas for the initiation of such a democratic system within our educational institutions:

1. Institutions should allow any qualified faculty and member of the public to run for paid full-time staff positions that influence admissions policies and procedures.

2. The qualification criteria should be designed in a way to not discriminate against any group of individuals while ensuring that selected individuals have the necessary educational background, experience, and required expertise to perform relevant tasks.

3. The qualifications must be determined based on the candidates' experience and expertise; the same or similar selection processes and tools should be used to select candidates. After all, why should an institution subject applicants to a screening process that the institution does not believe in itself?

4. Faculty should not be given any preference over members of the public to allow the election of best-suited individuals who may not be directly connected to the institutions.

5. Faculty, staff, students, and members of the public in the relevant geographical area served by the

institution should be notified in advance to vote for their choice of candidate from amongst the group of qualified candidates for each position.

6. The election process should be made simple, efficient and cost effective using a secure online voting platform.

7. The term of service for such positions must be limited to a maximum of 4–5 years per term and the total number of terms limited to 1 to 2, at most, for each individual.

8. Candidates should be limited in their ability to promote themselves, being required to use the same exact budget and platform for promoting their ideas.

9. A volunteer-based governing body composed of qualified members of the public and faculty should be elected using the same procedures as mentioned above, to oversee the conduct of the paid admissions staff; this governing body would have the power to eliminate any paid-position staff and/or other governing body members.

10. The governing body should review and vote for the suitability of the institutions' paid admissions staff and its members on a yearly basis.

11. The same process should be applied to other decision-makers within the institution, such as institution presidents, department deans, and program directors.

12. Lastly, and most importantly, no faculty, governing body member, or admissions staff should be allowed to seek the privatization of admissions-related research—either on their own or as part of a spin-off entity—to avoid conflict of interest and to

promote continuous research and development in the field. It is certainly not possible for a faculty, department director, or university to remain open to change if they have a vested interest in a spin-off organization.

When we combine a scientific admissions screening process with a democratic institution, we are bound to make profound improvements to the way we select applicants for their future roles. Transparency and accountability may cause temporary discomfort for admissions teams, but the long-term benefits vastly outweigh the short-term inconveniences. In this way, I believe it is possible to select applicants who are genuinely passionate about their future career. It is possible to save unnecessary time and cost. Above all, it is possible to promote diversity.

In the final two chapters, I will discuss the best practices for scoring applicants' responses and review sample questions and answers.

Chapter IV

How to Score Applicants' Responses

This is probably the most important part of the process; it is also possibly the part you want to keep as confidential as possible. Despite having spent a lot of time and money developing this system, I am going to share the system with you for free—I believe this is going to provide you 100 to 1,000 times the value you have spent in purchasing this book. However, to make it inaccessible to applicants, I have posted this online behind a gated web page, to limit access to admissions deans, directors, and other members of your admissions team. To gain access, please visit the following URL: sortsmart.io/scoring

Chapter V

Sample Questions and Answers

To train your evaluators, you must provide a comprehensive set of sample questions along with sample appropriate and inappropriate responses. The training should include instructions for evaluators to assess not just what the applicants are saying but how and in what order specific pieces of information are provided. To protect the contents of this chapter from applicants, I have posted it online behind a gated web page to limit access only to admissions deans, directors, and other members of your admissions team. To gain access, please visit sortsmart.io/scoring

Acknowledgments

I had the pleasure of working with several individuals who helped me build the strategies discussed in this book.

I would first like to thank the students who inspired me to spring into action. This includes many students from all imaginable walks of life who have gone on to become successful doctors, nurses, teachers, lawyers, dentists, and so forth. That alone is a testament to the fact that traditional admissions screening tools and practices are not built for today's world—according to such practices, most of these students would not have made it through the screening process.

While the students ignited this interest in me, my team members at both BeMo and SortSmart have fueled the fire and kept me going.

I am also privileged to have had the support of many good friends and family members, who helped me navigate challenging situations along the way.

Last, but not least, I would like to thank the admissions deans and directors who supported me and encouraged me to push ahead, even in times of uncertainty.

References:

Chapter I:

1. Rudan I, Rudan D, Campbell H et al. Inbreeding and risk of late onset complex disease. Journal of Medical Genetics. 2003; 40: 925–932.
2. Hermann A, Rammal H. The grounding of the 'flying bank'. Management Decision. 2010; 48(7):1048–1062.
3. Freeman RB, Huang W. Collaborating with People Like Me: Ethnic Coauthorship within the United States, in US High-Skilled Immigration in the Global Economy. Journal of Labor Economics. 2015; 33: S1.
4. Levine SS, Apfelbaum EP, Bernard M, Bartelt VL, Zajac EJ, Stark D. Ethnic diversity deflates price bubbles. PNAS. 2014, December 30; 111(52): 18524-18529.
5. Sommers, S. R. On racial diversity and group decision making: Identifying multiple effects of racial composition on jury

deliberations. Journal of Personality and Social Psychology.2006; 90(4): 597-612.

Chapter II:

6. Cyples W. Morality of the Doctrine of Averages. Cornhill Magazine. 1864: 218–224
7. Stahl S. The Evolution of the Normal Distribution. Mathematics Magazine. 2006; 79: 96–113
8. Sheynin OB. On the Mathematical Treatment of Astronomical Observations. Archives for the History of Exact Sciences. 1973; 11(2/3): 97–126
9. Quetelet LAJ. Lettres. Letters. 19–21.
10. Quetelet LAJ. Lettres. Letters. 20.
11. Quetelet LAJ. Treatise. 276.
12. Quetelet LAJ. Treatise. 99.
13. Stone M. The Owl and the Nightingale: The Quetelet/Nightingale Nexus. Chance 24. 2001; 4: 30–40.
14. Beirne P. Inventing Criminology. Albany: SUNY Press; 1993.
15. Wundt W. Theorie Der Sinneswahrnehmung. Leipzig: Winter'sche; 1862. p. xxv.
16. Maxwell JC. Illustrations of the Dynamical Theory of Gases. Philosophical Magazine 19. 1860: 19–32. Reprinted in The Scientific Papers of James Clerk Maxwell (Cambridge: Cambridge University Press; 1890, New York: Dover; 1952 and Courier Corporation; 2012)

17. Galton F. Memories of My Life. London: Methuen; 1908.
18. Sweeney G. Fighting for the Good Cause. Cambridge: Cambridge University Press, 2001. p. 35–49.
19. Galton F. Inquiries into Human Faculty and Its Development. London: Macmillan; 1883.
20. Galton F. Statistics by Intercomparison, with Remarks on the Law of Frequency of Error. Philosophical Magazine. 1875; 49: 33–46.
21. Galton F. Eugenics: Its Definition, Scope, and Aims. American Journal of Sociology. 1904. 10(1): 1–25.
22. Bulmer M, Galton F. Baltimore: JHU Press; 2004.p. 175.
23. Kanigel R. The one Best Way: Fredrick Winslow Taylor and the Enigma of Efficiency. Cambridge: MIT Press Books; 2005.
24. Hirschman C, Mogford E. Immigration and the American Industrial Revolution from 1880 to 1920. Social Science Research. 2009; 38(1):897–920.
25. Taylor Society. Scientific Management in American Industry. New York: Harper & Brothers; 1929. p. 28.
26. Taylor. Principles of Scientific Management. New York: Harper and Brothers; 1911. p. 83.
27. Taylor. Principles of Scientific Management. New York: Harper and Brothers; 1911. p. 25.
28. Derksen M. Turning Men into Machines? Scientific Management, Industrial Psychology, and the Human Factor. Journal of the History

of the Behavioral Sciences. 2014; 50(2): 148–1665.

29. Kanigel R. The one Best Way: Fredrick Winslow Taylor and the Enigma of Efficiency. Cambridge: MIT Press Books; 2005.

30. Taylor. Principles of Scientific Management. New York: Harper and Brothers; 1911.

31. Murnane RJ, Hoffman S. Graduations on the Rise. EducationNext [Internet]. Available from: https://www.educationnext.org/graduations-on-the-rise/; "Education" PBS. http://www.pbs.org/fmc/book/3education1.htm

32. Gates FT. The Country School of To-Morrow. Occasional Papers. 1913; 1: 6–10.

33. Gatto JT. The underground History of American Education. Odysseus Group. 2001: 222.

34. Mencken H L. The Little Red Schoolhouse. American Mercury. 1924, April: 504.

35. Joncich GM. The sane Positivist: A Biography of Edward L. Thorndike, Middletown: Wesleyan University Press; 1968.

36. Thorndike E. Educational Psychology: Mental Work and Fatigue and Individual Differences and Their Causes. New York: Columbia University; 1921. p.236.

37. Joncich GM. The sane Positivist: A Biography of Edward L. Thorndike, Middletown: Wesleyan University Press; 1968. p. 21–22.

38. Callahan RE. Education and the Cult of Efficiency. University of Chicago Press; 1964, chap. 5.

39. Wissler C. The correlation of Mental and Physical Tests. Psychological Review: Monograph Supplements. 1901; 3(6): p. i.

40. Thorndike RL, Hagen E. Ten Thousand Careers. New York: John Wiley & Sons; 1959.

41. Kobrin JL, et al. Validity of the SAT for Predicting First-Year College Grade Point Average. New York: College Board; 2008.

42. Gauer JL, Wolff JM, Jackson JB. Do MCAT scores predict USMLE scores? An analysis on 5 years of medical student data. Med Educ Online. 2016; 21: 31795.

43. Saguil A et al. Does the MCAT Predict Medical School and PGY-1 Performance? Military Medicine. 2015, April; 180(4): 4–11.

44. Carr SE, Celenza A, Puddey IB, Lake F. Relationships between academic performance of medical students and their workplace performance as junior doctors. BMC Med Educ. 2014; 14: 157.

45. Aguinis H., Culpepper SA, Pierce CA. Differential prediction generalization in college admissions testing. Journal of Educational Psychology. 2016; 108(7): 1045-1059.

46. Fadem B., Schuchman M, Simring S, The relationship between parental income and academic performance of medical students. Acad Med. 1995 Dec;70(12):1142-4.

47. The College Board. Total group profile Report [Internet]. 2013. Available from: http://secure-media.collegeboard.org/digitalServices/pdf/research/2013/TotalGroup-2013.pdf

48. Law School Admission Council. LSAT Performance With Regional, Gender, and Racial/Ethnic Breakdowns: 2007–2008 Through 2013–2014 Testing Years (TR 14-02) [Internet]. Available from: https://www.lsac.org/data-research/research/lsat-performance-regional-gender-and-racialethnic-breakdowns-2007-2008

49. Prideaux D, et al. Assessment for selection for the health care professions and specialty training: Consensus statement and recommendations from the Ottawa 2010 Conference. Medical Teacher. 2011; 33: 215–223.

50. Albanese MA, et al. Assessing personal qualities in medical school admissions. Acad Med, vol 78, 2003, pp. 313–321.

51. Wouters A, et al. A qualitative analysis of statements on motivation of applicants for medical school. BMC Medical Education. 2014; 14: 200

52. Shoda Y, et al. Persons in Contexts: Building a Science of the Individual. New York: Guildford Press; 2007.

53. Roberts, BW, Lejuez C, Krueger RF, Richards JM, Hill PL. What is conscientiousness and how can it be assessed? Developmental Psychology. 2014; 50(5): 1315–1330.

54. Dore, KL et al. Extending the interview to all medical school candidates--Computer-Based Multiple Sample Evaluation of Noncognitive Skills (CMSENS). Acad Med. 2009; 84(10):S9–S12.

55. Dore KL, et al. Adv in Health Sci Educ. 2017; 22: 327.
56. Kahneman D. Thinking, Fast and Slow. New York: Farrar, Straus and Giroux; 2011.
57. Kreiter CD, Yin P, Solow C, Brennan RL. Investigating the reliability of the medical school admissions interview. Adv Health Sci Educ Theory Pract. 2014; 9: 147–159.
58. Quintero A J, Segal LS, King TS, Black KP. The Personal Interview: Assessing the Potential for Personality Similarity to Bias the Selection of Orthopaedic Residents. Academic Medicine. 2009; 84: 1364–1372.
59. Eva KW, Rosenfeld J, Reiter HI, Norman, GR. An admissions OSCE: the multiple mini-interview. Med Edu. 2004; 38: 314–326.
60. Eva KW, Reiter HI, Rosenfeld J, Norman GR. The relationship between interviewers' characteristics and ratings assigned during a multiple mini-interview. Acad Med. 2004; 79: 602–609.
61. Eva KW, Reiter HI, Trinh K, Wasi P, Rosenfeld J, Norman GR. Predictive validity of the multiple mini-interview for selecting medical trainees. Med Educ. 2009; 43: 767–775.
62. Axelson RD, Kreiter CD. Rater and occasion impacts on the reliability of pre-admission assessments. Med Educ. 2009;43:1198–1202.
63. Dodson M, Crotty B, Prideaux D, Carne R, Ward A, de Leeuw E. The multiple mini-interview: how long is long enough? Med Educ. 2009;43:168–174.

64. Eva KW, Reiter HI, Rosenfeld J, Norman GR. The relationship between interviewers' characteristics and ratings assigned during a multiple mini-interview. Acad Med. 2004;79:602–609.

65. Gafni N, Moshinsky A, Eisenberg O, Zeigler D, Ziv A. Reliability estimates: behavioural stations and questionnaires in medical school admissions. Med Educ. 2012;46:277–288.

66. Finlayson HC, Townson AF. Resident selection for a physical medicine and rehabilitation program feasibility and reliability of the multiple mini-interview. Am J Phys Med Rehabil. 2011;90:330–335.

67. Ziv A, Rubin O, Moshinsky A, Gafni N, Kotler M, Dagan Y, Lichtenberg D, Mekori YA, Mittelman M. MOR: a simulation-based assessment centre for evaluating the personal and interpersonal qualities of medical school candidates. Med Educ. 2008;42:991–998.

68. Tiller D, O'Mara D, Rothnie I, Dunn S, Lee L, Roberts C. Internet-based multiple mini-interviews for candidate selection for graduate entry programmes. Med Educ. 2013;47:801–810.

69. Jean-Michel Leduc, Richard Rioux, Robert Gagnon, Christian Bourdy & Ashley Dennis (2017) Impact of sociodemographic characteristics of applicants in multiple mini-interviews, Medical Teacher, 39:3, 285-294.

70. Jerant A, Fancher T, Fenton JJ, Fiscella K, Sousa F, Franks P, Henderson M. How Medical School Applicant Race, Ethnicity, and

Socioeconomic Status Relate to Multiple Mini-Interview-Based Admissions Outcomes: Findings From One Medical School. Acad Med. 2015 Dec;90(12):1667-74.

71. Ross M, Walker I, Cooke L, Raman M, Ravani P, Coderre S, McLaughlin K. Are Female Applicants Rated Higher Than Males on the Multiple Mini-Interview? Findings From the University of Calgary. Acad Med. 2017 Jun;92(6):841-846.

72. Fern Juster. What Impact Does An SJT Have On Diversity Recruitment At A US Allopathic Medical School With A Commitment To Diversity And Inclusion? April 2016 Canadian Conference on Medical Education (CCME), Montreal, Canada.

73. Jerant A1, Griffin E, Rainwater J, Henderson M, Sousa F, Bertakis KD, Fenton JJ, Franks P. Does applicant personality influence multiple mini-interview performance and medical school acceptance offers? Academic Medicine. 2012 September; 87(9): 1250–1259.

74. Henderson MC, Kelly CJ, Griffin E, Hall TR, Jerant A, Peterson EM, Rainwater JA, Sousa FJ, Wofsy D, Franks P. Medical School Applicant Characteristics Associated With Performance in Multiple Mini-Interviews Versus Traditional Interviews: A Multi-Institutional Study. Academic Medicine. 2018, July; 93(7): 1029–1034.

75. Harold R, Kevin E. Vive la Différence: The Freedom and Inherent Responsibilities When Designing and Implementing Multiple Mini-

Interviews. Academic Medicine. 2018, July; 93(7):969–971.

76. Grbic D, Jones DJ, Case ST. The Role of Socioeconomic Status in Medical School Admissions: Validation of a Socioeconomic Indicator for Use in Medical School Admissions. Academic Medicine. 2015, July; 90(7):953–960.

77. Capers Q, Clinchot D, McDougle L, Greenwald SG. Implicit Racial Bias in Medical School Admissions. Academic Medicine. 2017, March; 92(3):365–369.

78. AAMC Survey [Internet]. 2017. Available from: https://www.aamc.org/download/481784/data/2 017gqallschoolssummaryreport.pdf

Chapter III:

Rule #2:

79. Deci EL, Richard RM. Intrinsic Motivation and Self-determination in Human Behavior. New York (N.Y.): Plenum; 1985.

80. Ryan RM, Deci, EL. Self-determination theory: Basic psychological needs in motivation, development, and wellness. New York, NY, US: Guilford Press; 2017.

81. Csikszentmihalyi M. Flow: The Psychology of Optimal Experience. New York: Harper & Row; 1990.

82. Fredrick CM, Ryan RM. Differences in motivation for sport and exercise and their

relations with participation and mental health. Journal of Sport Behavior. 1993; 16(3): 124-146.

83. Ryan RM, Deci EL. Active human nature: Self-determination theory and the promotion and maintenance of sport, exercise, and health. In M.S. Haggar & N. L. Chatzisarantis (Eds.), Intrinsic motivation and self-determination in exercise and sport. Champaign, IL: Human Kinetics; 2007. p. 1-19.

84. Gill DL, Gross JB, Huddleston S. Participation motives in youth sports. International Journal of Sport Psychology. 1983; 14: 1-14.

85. Gould D, Feltz D, Weiss MR. Motives for participating in competitive youth swimming. International Journal of Sport Psychology. 1985; 16(2): 126-140.

86. Raedeke TD. Is athlete burnout more than just stress? A sport commitment perspective. Journal of Sport and Exercise Psychology. 1997;19: 396-417.

87. Orlick TD, Mosher R. Extrinsic awards and participant motivation in sport-related task. International Journal of Sport Psychology. 1978; 9: 27-39.

88. Powers TA, Koestner R,Gorin AA. Autonomy support from family and friends and weight loss in college women. Families, Systems, and Health. 2008; 26(4): 404-416.

89. Senecal C, Nouwen A, White D. Motivation and dietary self-care in adults with diabetes: Are self-efficacy and autonomous self-regulation

complementary or competing constructs? Health Psychology. 2000;19(5): 452-457.

90. Diener E, Emmons RA, Larsen RJ, Griffin S. The satisfaction with Life Scale. Journal of Personaltiy Assessment. 1985; 49(1): 71-75.

91. Williams GC, McGregor H, Sharp D, Kouides RW, et al. A self-determination multiple risk intervention trial to improve smokers' health. Journal of General Internal Medicine. 2006; 21(12): 1288-1294.

92. Williams GC, McGregor H, Sharp D, Levesque C, et al. Testing a self-determination theory intervention for motivating tobacco cessation: Supporting autonomy and competence in a clinical trial. Health Psychology. 2006; 25(1): 91-101.

93. Halvari AEM, Halvari H. Motivational predictors of change in oral health: An experimental test of self-determination theory. Motivation and Emotion. 2006; 30(4): 294-306.

94. Wolfe GR, Stewart JE, Maeder LA, Hartz GW. (Use of dental coping beliefs scale to measure cognitive changes following oral hygiene interventions. Community Dentistry and Oral Epidemiology. 1996; 24(1): 37-41.

95. Munster-Halvari AE, Halvari H, Bjornebekk G, Deci EL. Motivation and anxiety for dental treatment: Testing a self-determination theory model of self-care behavior and dental clinic attendance. Motivation and Emotions. 2010; 34(1): 15-33.

96. Munster-Halvari AE, Halvari H, Bjornebekk G, Deci EL. Motivation for dental home care:

Testing a self-determination theory model. Journal of Applied Social Psychology. 2012; 42(1): 1-39.

97. Munster-Halvari AE, Halvari H, Bjornebekk G, Deci EL. Oral health and dental well-being: Testing a self-determination theory model. Journal of Applied Spychology. 2013; 43(2): 275-292.

98. Williams GC, Rodin GC, Ryan RM, Grolnick WS, Deci EL. Autonomous regulation and long-term medication adherence in adult outpatients. Health Psychology. 1998; 17(3): 269-276.

99. Williams GC, Deci EL. The importance of supporting autonomy in medical education. Annals of Internal Medicine. 1998; 129(4): 303-308.

100. What Day Is the Most Productive? Tuesday! AccountingWeb [Internet]. Available from: https://www.accountingweb.com/practice/growth/what-day-is-the-most-productive-tuesday

101. Monday 'most common for sickness'. BBC News on Mercer survey [Internet]. Available from: http://news.bbc.co.uk/2/hi/health/8347332.stm

102. Fernet C, Austin S, Valerand RJ. The effects of work motivation on employee exhaustion and commitment: An extension of the JD-R model. Work and Stress: An International Journal of Work, Health, and Organizations. 2012; 26(3): 213-229.

103. Otis N, Pelletier LG. A motivational model of daily hassles, physical symptoms and future work intentions among police officers. Journal

of Applied Social Psychology. 2005; 35(10): 2193-2214.

104. Levesque M, Blais MR, Hess U. Motivation, discretionary organisational attitudes and well-being in an African environment: When does duty call? Canadian Journal of Behavioral Science/Revue Canadienne des Sciences du Comportement. 2004; 36(4): 321-332.

105. Nie Y, Chua BL, Yeung AS, Ryan RM, Chan WY. The importance of autonomy support and the mediating role of work motivation for well-being: Self-determination theory in a Chinese work organization. International Journal of Psychology. 2015; 50(4): 245-255.

106. Becker TE, et al. Dual Commitments to Organizations and Professions: Different Motivational Pathways to Productivity. Journal of Management. 2018, March; 44(3): 1202–1225.

107. Fernet C, Guay F, Senécal C, Austin S. Predicting intraindividual changes in teacher burnout: The role of Perceived work environment and motivational factors. Teaching and Teacher Education. 2012.

108. Trépanier SG, et al. Workplace Psychological Harassment in Canadian Nurses: A Descriptive Study. Journal of Health Psychology. 2013, March; 18(3): 383–396.

109. Vansteenkiste M, Neyrinck B, Niemiec CP, Soenens B, Witte H, Broeck A. On the relations among work value orientations, psychological need satisfaction and job outcomes: A self-determination theory approach. Journal of

Occupational and Organizational Psychology. 2007; 80: 251-277.

110. Van den Broeck A, Vansteenkiste M, Lens W, De Witte H. Unemployed Individuals' Work Values and Job Flexibility: An Explanation from Expectancy-Value Theory and Self-Determination Theory. Applied Psychology. 2010; 59: 296-317.

111. Fernet C, Guay F, Senécal C. Adjusting to job demands: The role of work self-determination and job control in predicting burnout. Journal of Vocational Behavior. 2004; 65: 39-56.

112. Danner FW, Edward L. A Cognitive-Developmental Approach to the Effects of Rewards on Intrinsic Motivation. Child Development. 1981; 52(3): 1043–1052.

113. Richard R, James PC, Robert PW. Emotions in nondirected text learning. Learning and Individual Differences - LEARN INDIVID DIFFER. 1990; 2: 1-17.

114. Taylor G, Jungert T, Mageau G, Schattke K, Dedic H, Rosenfield S, Koestner R. A self-determination theory approach to predicting school achievement over time: The unique role of intrinsic motivation. Contemporary Educational Psychology. 2014; 39.

115. Froiland J, Worrell F. Intrinsic motivation, learning goals, engagement, and achievement in a diverse high school. Psychology in the Schools. 2016; 53.

116. Vansteenkiste Maarten, Sierens Eli, Goossens L, Soenens B, Dochy F, Mouratidis T, Aelterman N, Haerens L, Beyers W.

Identifying configurations of perceived teacher autonomy support and structure: Associations with self-regulated learning, motivation and problem behavior. Learning and Instruction. 2012; 22: 431-439.

117. Aaron BE, Deci E. The effects of instructors' autonomy support and students' autonomous motivation on learning organic chemistry: A self-determination theory perspective. Science Education. 2000; 84: 740 -756.

118. Williams GC, Deci E.L. Internalization of biopsychosocial values by medical students: A test of self-determination theory. Journal of Personality and Social Psychology. 1996; 70(4): 767-779.

119. Williams G, Saizow R, Ross L, Deci E. Motivation underlying career choice for internal medicine and surgery. Social Science & Medicine. 1998; 45: 1705-1713.

120. Sheldon K, Krieger, LS. Understanding the Negative Effects of Legal Education on Law Students: A Longitudinal Test of Self-Determination Theory. Personality & social psychology bulletin. 2007; 33: 883-97.

121. Grolnick W, Ryan R. Autonomy in Children's Learning: An Experimental and Individual Difference Investigation. Journal of personality and social psychology. 1987; 52. 890-898.

122. Benware CA, Deci, E. Quality of Learning With an Active Versus Passive Motivational Set. American Educational Research Journal. 1984; 21: 755-765.

123. Hout M, Elliott SW. Incentives and Test-Based Accountability in Education. Washington, DC: The National Academies Press. 2011.
124. Deci EL, et al. Extrinsic Rewards and Intrinsic Motivation in Education: Reconsidered Once Again. Review of Educational Research. 2001, March; 71(1): 1–27.

Rule #3:

125. Smither JW, London M, Reilly R. Does Performance Improve Following Multisource Feedback? A Theoretical Model, Meta-Analysis, and Review of Empirical Findings. Personnel Psychology. 2005; 58: 33 - 66.
126. von Guenthner S, Hammermeister J. Exploring relations of wellness and Athletic Coping Skills of collegiate athletes: Implications for sport performance. Psychological reports. 2008;101: 1043-1049.
127. Shannahan K, Bush A, Shannahan R. Are your salespeople coachable? How salesperson coachability, trait competitiveness, and transformational leadership enhance sales performance. Journal of the Academy of Marketing Science. 2012; 41.
128. George P, Reis S, Dobson M, Nothnagle M. Using a Learning Coach to Develop Family Medicine Residents' Goal-Setting and Reflection Skills. Journal of graduate medical education. 2013; 5: 289-293.

129. Palter VN, Beyfuss KA, Jokhio AR, Ryzynski A, Ashamalla S. Peer coaching to teach faculty surgeons an advanced laparoscopic skill: A randomized controlled trial. Surgery. 2016.

130. Theeboom T, Beersma B, van Vianen AEM. Does coaching work? A meta-analysis on the effects of coaching on individual level outcomes in an organizational context, The Journal of Positive Psychology. 2013.

Rule #4:

131. Duckworth A, Weir D, Tsukayama E & Kwok D. Who Does Well in Life? Conscientious Adults Excel in Both Objective and Subjective Success. Frontiers in psychology. 2012; 3: 356.

132. Poropat, A. A Meta-Analysis of the Five-Factor Model of Personality and Academic Performance. Psychological bulletin. 2009; 135: 322-38.

133. Roberts, BW et al. Compensatory conscientiousness and health in older couples. Psychological science. 2009; 20(5): 553-9.

134. Deary IJ, et al. Intelligence and Personality as Predictors of Illness and Death: How Researchers in Differential Psychology and Chronic Disease Epidemiology Are Collaborating to Understand and Address Health Inequalities. Psychological Science in the Public Interest. 2010, August; 11(2): 53–79

135. Kern M, Friedman SH. Personality and Pathways of Influence on Physical Health.

Personality and Pathways of Influence on Physical Health. 2011; 5: 76-87.

136. Barrick MR, Mount MK, Judge TA. Personality and Performance at the Beginning of the New Millennium: What Do We Know and Where Do We Go Next?. International Journal of Selection and Assessment. 2001; 9: 9-30.

137. Roberts BW, et al. The Power of Personality: The Comparative Validity of Personality Traits, Socioeconomic Status, and Cognitive Ability for Predicting Important Life Outcomes. Perspectives on Psychological Science. 2007, Dec;2(4): 313–345.

138. Roberts BW, Jackson JJ, Fayard JV, Edmonds G, Meints J. Conscientiousness. Handbook of Individual Differences in Social Behavior, eds M. Leary and R. Hoyle. NewYork,NY:Guilford); 2009.p. 369–381.

139. Jensen-Campbell LA, Malcolm KT. The importance of conscientiousness in adolescent interpersonal relationships. Pers. Soc. Psychol. Bull. 2007; 33: 368–383.

140. Diener E, Biswas-Diener, R. Happiness: Unlocking the Mysteries of Psychological Wealth. Malden: Blackwell Publishing. 2008.

Rule #6:

141. Capraro V, Schulz J, Rand D. Time pressure increases honesty in a sender-receiver deception game. 2018.

Rule #7:

142. Lewis JR. Multipoint scales: Mean and median differences and observed significance levels, International Journal of Human–Computer Interaction. 1993; 5(4): 383–392.
143. Preston CC, Colman AM. Optimal number of response categories in rating scales: reliability, validity, discriminating power, and respondent preferences, Acta Psychologica. 2000; 104(1): 1-15.
144. Finstad K. Response Interpolation and Scale Sensitivity: Evidence Against 5-Point Scales. 2009: 5.

Rule #8:

145. Cozby PC, Bates S. Methods in Behavioral Research. New York, NY: McGraw-Hill; 2017.
146. Moskal B, Leydens J. Scoring Rubric Development: Validity and Reliability. Practical Assessment Research and Evaluation. 2000: 7.
147. Moss-Racusin CA et al. Science faculty's subtle gender biases favor male students. Proceedings of the National Academy of Sciences of the United States of America. 2012; 109(41): 16474–16479.
148. Dechief D, Oreopoulos P. Why Do Some Employers Prefer to Interview Matthew, but Not Samir? New Evidence from Toronto, Montreal, and Vancouver. SSRN Electronic Journal. 2012.

Rule #9:

149. Cozby PC, Bates S. Methods in Behavioral Research. New York, NY: McGraw-Hill; 2017.
150. Moskal B and Leydens J. Scoring Rubric Development: Validity and Reliability. Practical Assessment Research and Evaluation. 2000:7.

About the author:

Behrouz **Moemeni** is the founder and CEO at SortSmart® Candidate Selection (SortSmart.io). A scientist by training with a PhD in Immunology from the University of Toronto, he is known for creating motivation-based admissions screening.

Dr. Moemeni is one of the most sought-after admissions screening experts. His scientific approach to applicant screening along with his admissions screening software are designed to help institutions select top-performing applicants while promoting diversity.

His motivation-based admissions screening strategy has appeared in *Diverse Issues in Higher Education*, *University World News*, *CMAJ News*, and *Nature Jobs*. He regularly presents thought-provoking presentations to an international audience including appearances at TEDx, WLUBrantford, and Beyond Sciences Initiative. His website is behrouzmoemeni.com.